GILGAMESH

The Archetypal Significance of

Gilgamesh

A Modern Ancient Hero

by
Rivkah Schärf Kluger

edited by
H. Yehezkel Kluger

DAIMON
VERLAG

ACKNOWLEDGMENTS

The editor wishes to express his grateful acknowledgment to Dr. Aryeh Maidenbaum, Executive Director of the C.G. Jung Institute of New York, for his friendly efforts in seeing to the defrayal of the costs of publication, and for both his material as well as moral contribution to the work. My warm thanks are also due to Dr. Maury Leibovitz for his generous support through the Maury Leibovitz Foundation. It is a singular pleasure to acknowledge indebtedness to the Erlo van Waveren Foundation for its valuable grant, in view of the mutual regard which existed between the author and the late Mr. van Waveren. My thanks and gratitude also go to Judy Maidenbaum for her kind participation in the funding of the book. Not least, thanks are due to the publisher, Dr. Robert Hinshaw, whose warm personal interest and participation in the preparatory work far exceeded the usual professional connection, and whose support and encouragement over the years extended even to care and concern for the author and editor (by his wife Lela, too, who thus also merits acknowledgment and thanks).

HYK

Gilgamesh by Rivkah Schärf Kluger is a result of the joint efforts of the C.G. Jung Foundation of New York and Daimon Verlag of Switzerland to publish significant works in the field of Analytical Psychology.

The publisher and editor acknowledge with gratitude the providers of the illustrations used in this book.

Cover design by Hanspeter Kälin. Cover illustration: Gilgamesh – a giant bas-relief of the lion-conquering hero as guardian of the palace of Sargon II. Photograph of the author by James Kirsch.

GILGAMESH

CONTENTS

LIST OF ILLUSTRATIONS

FOREWORD

When Rivkah Schärf presented her doctoral dissertation in 1948,* C.G. Jung immediately noticed that she had a talent for research, along with unfailing conscientiousness. Thus he encouraged her to begin working on a topic he had particularly loved since his early research in mythology: *Gilgamesh.* She naturally accepted his suggestion gladly, unaware of the enormity of this endeavor, unaware that the task of providing a psychological commentary on the Gilgamesh Epic would continue to occupy her for the rest of her life. Her background in the comparative history of religion was a precious requisite, and she proceeded leaving no stone unturned. But interpreting the text in terms of Jungian psychology was to be her own unique contribution, since in the enormous already existing literature about Gilgamesh, there was almost nothing of a psychological nature to be found. The reader will therefore understand that in her own text, the author quotes only books and articles giving the archaeological and philological foundations of the text of the epic.

Rivkah Kluger correctly calls the Gilgamesh Epic a myth. When it comes to interpreting myths, fairy tales and religious material, we already have numerous examples from Jung

* This dissertation was first published in German: "Die Gestalt des Satans im Alten Testament" (Rascher Verlag, Zurich, 1948) and later in English: "Satan in the Old Testament" (Northwestern University Press, Evanston, 1967).

himself, demonstrating the application of his ideas to the elaboration of such time-honored texts. It is here that the author's talent is particularly rewarding, as she most meticulously takes into account the impressive fact that she is working with a myth: a venerable myth that has come down to us from about four thousand years ago. This requires a never-failing awareness of the particular cultural conditions under which it originated, i.e., the frame of mind peculiar to those people in their own period of the world's history. Only then can we appreciate the process of individuation as it existed in that moment of time. For all true myth, as Jung has shown, describes in essence the process of individuation of its hero. Rivkah Kluger's amplifications clearly demonstrate her deep respect for these processes, for which we are especially grateful. Bearing all this in mind, we can regard Rivkah Kluger's *Gilgamesh* as a classic study of an analysis of individuation.

When reading this book we should be aware, however, that it had to be posthumously composed, a tremendous labor of care and love by Rivkah's husband, Dr. Yehezkel Kluger, compiled from the many *disiecta membra*, tape recordings, lectures and seminars, given in the old as well as the new world over a period of many many years. Let us be grateful to him for making this masterful work accessible, and for having thus erected this beautiful monument both to her and to Jungian psychology in general.

Prof. Dr. C.A. Meier

PREFACE

The following is the posthumous publication of a major work undertaken by the author at the instigation of C.G. Jung after he had included her monograph "The Figure of Satan in the Old Testament" in his book *Symbolik des Geistes,* which appeared in 1948. She had lectured on the subject at the Psychologische Club Zürich while Jung was still an active participant, and also since then, at various other cities. A 1962 seminar given at the C.G. Jung Institut-Zürich was recorded, and this book consists of the transcription of those tapes, augmented from her notes for her lectures.

The great beauty and depth of the Gilgamesh Epic makes it a unique instrument for learning about the human soul. The seminar was given as part of the analytical training for candidates, and illuminates the significance of myths for the understanding of the growth of consciousness and the development of religion, in the light of the processes of the unconscious. Also, the material and style of presentation is highlighted in accordance with its pertinence for our current age. Its applicability in meeting the concerns, needs and problems of modern man is demonstrated by illustrations from dreams and case material, as well as personal recollections. It was decided to print the material in the form in which she delivered it, as with the Jung seminars, to permit the reader to enjoy so far as the written word can convey it, the liveliness and enthusiasm with which she imbued her lectures, while nevertheless adhering to her high level of scholarly precision. A condensed version of the material was published as "Einige psychologische Aspekte des Gilgamesch-Epos" in the 1975 Jung Centennial edition of *Analytische Psychologie,* Vol. 6, Nr. 3.

It is regrettable that her illness, and her death in December of 1987, prevented her participation in the final preparation of her work for publication, but the editor, who had frequent and full discussions of the material with her over a period of many years, hopes to have succeeded in permitting her own words to convey her knowledge and depth to the reader.

H. Yehezkel Kluger
Haifa, June 4, 1989

INTRODUCTION

1. Myths are "Soul-Matter"

The Gilgamesh Epic, a masterpiece of world literature, is considered to be one of the oldest epics in the world. It is called an epic, but as we shall see, it is really a myth. In order to be able to understand a myth, it seems to me to be necessary to have an *historical* point of view from two perspectives, so to speak, an outer and an inner one. The outer one concerns the necessity to understand the historical *form* in which the archetypes appear, the historical background to which the myth is related – in our case, the Babylonian culture and religion. The inner aspect concerns the essential problems of the time, with which that particular epoch struggled consciously, or in which it was unconsciously involved. Although this is primarily a scientific task, I believe that it is nevertheless a matter of immediate necessity for us to understand such *documents humains* in relation to our own life, for all the ages live in us, and we cannot really understand ourselves unless we know our spiritual roots.

What particular age and what spiritual contents are evoked in us by the unconscious is, to a certain extent, a question of individual fate. Since Western culture is based to a great extent on Judaism and Christianity, Babylonian culture as one of their roots may be looked upon as of immediate psychological interest to us all. The archetypes live in their realm, beyond time and space. This builds the bridge of understanding between men of all ages, and makes it possible to realize that we ourselves with our essential problems are bound up in the continuity of the eternal problems of mankind, as they are mirrored in myths. But the form in which the archetypes appear, their garments so to speak, depends on the historical conditions: the symbols in which they appear change. In the human being these changes correspond to the development of human consciousness. Thus the myths, in my opinion, represent not only eternal archetypal events, but a certain level of the development of human consciousness. During my work on this remarkably rich material this connection thrust itself more and more into my mind, so that I should like to define it as the basic idea, as the starting point of my attempt to explain this myth.

It was only in 1872 that scholars first became aware of this myth, when the English Assyriologist George Smith made public "The Chaldean Account of the Deluge," as he titled his translation of the eleventh tablet of the epic. Excavations at Kouyunjik, the old Nineveh, uncovered many fragments, which were then brought to the British Museum in London. Further finds, there and elsewhere, have occupied scholars in Europe and America. Gilgamesh, King of Uruk – the Biblical Erech – had first been identified with the hunter Nimrod, to whose realm, according to Genesis 10:10, Erech belonged. Only later did it become clear, through finds of older Sumerian material, that this was not the case. As the American Sumerologist, Samuel Noah Kramer, has demonstrated, the epic contains and combines elements of older Sumerian myths, integrating the earlier disconnected material into a single plot. The oldest Sumerian fragments, found in the Mesopotamian cities Nippur, Kish, and Ur, go back to the fourth millennium B.C.E. The name Gilgamesh was shown to be not Semitic, but Sumerian. The Sumerians were the oldest inhabitants of Mesopotamia of whom we know. So far their language has not been linked up with any other. They were the inventors of cuneiform (wedge-shaped) script, which was taken over by their successors, the Babylonians and Assyrians, together with the whole Sumerian culture. But these gave to the Sumerian culture their own particular stamp, and typical Semitic conceptions were likewise brought into the Gilgamesh Epic.

The epic as such is the creation of the Semitic Babylonians and its first fragments belong to the so-called Old Babylonian period, i.e., during the dynasty of Hammurabi, in the first half of the second millennium B.C.E. But this first Old Babylonian version is very fragmentary. Fortunately later copies and further elaborations of these fragments were found in the excavations at Nineveh, in the library of Assurbanipal, the last great Assyrian king, who reigned in the 7th century B.C.E. The latest version is written on twelve clay tablets and is the result of at least 1800 to 2000 years of work on the epic. Further fragments have since come to light which contain valuable additions to the damaged and incomplete text. Among them are also translations into Hittite and Hurrian. An Akkadian fragment dating from approximately the 14th century B.C.E., was also found in Meggido, Canaan, thus prior to the Israelite settlement there. These finds show how widespread the Gilgamesh Epic was, from the south of Babylonia up to Asia Minor, and in what high esteem it must have been held.

We may assume that, like other myths and folk-tales, the Gilgamesh Epic was originally conveyed to the people orally, recited by rhapsodists, as indicated by its style and frequent repetitive passages, impressing the message on the soul of the people, where it underwent further development and transformations.

Just which particular sources were brought together, and how, does not seem to me to be a mere matter of chance. The author or authors of this composition must have had the feeling that it made sense, as did those who accepted it in this form through the centuries. The combining factor can be found in the creative unconscious of those who brought the different materials into connection with each other. Thus to attempt a psychological interpretation of this ancient epic, so pregnant with meaning, seems to be a justified endeavor. Myths are "soul-matter," like dreams, and call for symbolic understanding and translation.

Since Jung's discovery of the collective unconscious and its contents, the archetypes (the basic typical forms of human thought, feelings, and reactions which underlie and determine the boundless variety of individual experiences), new light has fallen on the essence of myths. Finding mythological motifs turning up in the dreams of modern man, Jung recognized that myths, like dreams, are manifestations of the unconscious. It became evident in practice that bringing in mythological parallels as amplification of archetypal dreams not only deepens the understanding of the latter, but also leads to a further psychological understanding of the myth. His path-breaking work, *Symbols of Transformation*, laid the foundation for a wide field of psychological research on myths and their relevance for modern man.

2. Myths and the Growth of Human Consciousness

Myths, so far as their origin is concerned, are, like dreams, spontaneous expressions of the unconscious. Just as dreams, as Jung has shown, are related in a compensatory way to the current state of the consciousness of the dreamer, so the myths, we may assume, are related to the collective state of consciousness of a certain time. But who is its dreamer? We could presume to say the collective ego of the tribe or populace, that is, the commonly held beliefs and attitudes, the collective consciousness. But this leads to another question which is important for the interpretation of a myth taken as a collective dream: there is no individual ego to whom one could turn for associations to help establish the context in which the dream occurs. How can we interpret a myth without the particular point of reference we have for individual dreams in the person of the dreamer? Here the only context available is the culture of the time in which the myth arose and was valued. Myths are therefore like reflections or mirrorings of certain cultural situations of mankind, and like great, archetypal individual dreams, they contain deep intuitions and anticipations of further developments, and thus they can be considered as *milestones in the development of human consciousness.*

When we interpret an individual dream we can look at the figures occurring in it (apart from that of the dreamer himself, which generally represents his ego) under the aspect of their so-called objective or subjective significance, the latter referring to the inner, largely unconscious, aspect of the dreamer's personality. The more collective and archetypal a dream is, the more the subjective level of interpretation suggests itself. This is all the more the case with a myth, where, to begin with, there is no individual ego of a dreamer to which to refer. But there are individuals, divine and human, appearing and acting in the myth, and they can be understood as aspects of the projected wholeness of the human psyche, be it individual or carried by the community, the collective. In the hero myth in particular, there is one character, the hero, who is the actor in a continuous sequence of events. The hero can, therefore, be considered as the anticipation of a development of ego-consciousness, and what he goes through in the myth as an indication of the process of moving toward the wholeness which is implicit and innate in the psyche; in the individual, the individuation process. That is apparently why archetypal dreams occur frequently in crucial times in our lives, in states of transition. Old myths can then become not only valuable amplifications for such dreams, but the very key for their understanding. For we are consciously or unconsciously living or being lived by archetypal patterns, and it is mythological images which are usually behind the deepest experiences of *meaning* in our lives.

It doesn't seem to be mere chance that in modern times publications on the Gilgamesh Epic have multiplied, not only in the field of Assyriology, but also in poetic works, literary compositions, and artistic representations. It is as though our time has to find its own understanding of such statements of eternal human concern, in order to find the specific meaning or place of our own epoch in the process of a growing enlargement of consciousness, which is the ultimate meaning and goal of myth. As Jung has said in his introduction to "The Psychology of the Child Archetype" (par. 267):

> "... we can never legitimately cut loose from our archetypal foundations unless we are prepared to pay the price of a neurosis, any more than we can rid ourselves of our body and its organs without committing suicide. If we cannot deny the archetypes or otherwise neutralize them, we are confronted, at every new stage in the differentiation of consciousness to which civilization attains, with the task of finding a new *interpretation* appropriate to this stage, in order to connect the life of the past that still exists in us with the life of the present, which threatens to slip away from it. If this link-up does not take place, a kind of rootless consciousness comes into being no longer oriented to the past, a consciousness which succumbs helplessly to all manner of suggestions, and, in practice, is susceptible to psychic epidemics."

To how great an extent "the life of the past still exists in us" we shall discover as we pursue our psychological investigation of the Gilgamesh Epic. Because of the broken and damaged state of the tablets the text has many gaps, which leave questions open, the solution of which must await the finding of additional fragments of the epic. But the fascination exerted by the Gilgamesh Epic, rooted in its psychological depth, overrides these obstacles. It requires but little phantasy and intuition to fill the lacunae, for enough of the text has remained to give a feeling of meaningful continuity to the happenings in the story, and of the wholeness of an inner process behind the myth.

In working on the material I have used all the available

translations in German, French, Dutch, and, in English, R. Campbell Thompson's poetic rendition in English hexameter, E. A. Speiser's translation in *Ancient Near Eastern Texts Relating to the Old Testament*, and Alexander Heidel's *The Gilgamesh Epic and Old Testament Parallels*. This last is the text I will follow for the most part. Heidel gives a thorough and good introduction to the text, and brings in full the parallel Old Babylonian and Hittite texts where there are gaps in the standard version. I do not agree with his ideas about the Old Testament parallels, and this part has been rather generally criticized, but as far as the text and its publication goes, it is considered to be good, carefully done, and reliable.

I am sorry to say that my study of the Akkadian language and cuneiform script have not advanced far enough to enable me to base my investigations on the original text. I am quite aware that I may also have overlooked some psychological facts which could have revealed themselves only to one possessing a more profound knowledge of the language. I must therefore plead for your indulgence in this respect. But the relatively great number of scientifically valued translations seemed to me to warrant the attempt at a psychological explanation.

I

THE WALL OF URUK

1. Gilgamesh, Two-Thirds God

Let us now turn to the text. (In order to make for smoother reading I will omit the various kinds of brackets used to indicate damaged texts and restorations, but will maintain the dots indicating gaps in the text.) Tablet I contains an introduction which praises the hero, an indication that the epic was first told by rhapsodists, as mentioned earlier, who first announced the qualities of the hero they were going to praise.

> *He who saw everything, of him learn, O my land;*
> *He who knew all the lands, him will I praise.*
> *.... together....*
> *.... wisdom, who everything....*
> *He saw secret things and obtained knowledge of hidden things.*
> *He brought tidings of the days before the flood*
> *He went on a long journey, became weary and worn;*
> *He engraved on a table of stone all the travail.*
>
> (Tabl. I, col. i, lines 1-8, Heidel p. 16)

This beginning really anticipates the end. It shows what the hero Gilgamesh became by virtue of his deeds and experiences. This brief span of the path of his development impressively brings to light the quality of destiny in the fate of the hero. Then the laudation of the hero turns back to the great deed of his youth.

He built the wall of Uruk, the enclosure,
Of holy Eanna, the sacred storehouse.
Behold its outer wall, whose brightness is like that of copper!
Yea, look upon its inner wall, which none can equal!
Take hold of the threshold, which is from of old!
Approach Eanna, the dwelling of Ishtar,
Which no later king, no man, can equal!

(lines 9-15, Heidel p. 16f)

Uruk, the Biblical Erech mentioned among other Mesopotamian cities in Genesis 10:10, was the city-state of which Gilgamesh was king. Eanna was the temple of the sky-god Anu, head of the Sumerian pantheon, and more importantly, of his daughter Ishtar, that most powerful goddess who overshadowed him, of whom we shall speak more later. The superhuman quality of Gilgamesh is especially evident in the description of his appearance:

The valiant god ... perfected his form....
The heavenly Shamash granted him comeliness;
Adad granted him heroism....
The form of Gilgamesh the great gods made surpassing.
Eleven cubits was his height; the breadth of his chest was nine
                                                  spans.
The length of his ... was three ...
....

(lines 4-9, Hittite version, Heidel p. 17)

Two-thirds of him is god and one-third of him is man.
The form of his body none can match.
....
The onslaught of his weapons has no equal.

(Tabl. I, col. ii, lines 1-9, Heidel p. 18)

This description shows Gilgamesh as a typical *mythological* hero. The mythological hero is virtually always partly divine and partly human. This seems to me to point to the fact that the hero is an intuitive anticipation of the development towards human consciousness of the divine in man. His divinity is indicated by his superhuman measurements and qualities, and the extent of his deeds and his wisdom are a measure of his achievement in fulfilling the cultural task awaiting him. The myth, thus, is always ahead of the actual level of consciousness of the time, and so the hero is the symbol or carrier of a process of change: for modern man, the process of individuation. His struggles with threatening powers, in which he is helped or encouraged by positive counter powers, results in the establishment of a new relationship between them, in our terms, the relationship between consciousness and the unconscious.

The typical hero, as in the more familiar Greek myths, is usually half human, half divine. As to why Gilgamesh is two-thirds divine and only one-third human, I would suggest that in the archaic time in which this myth arose, the level of developed consciousness was lower, and so the hero, the representative of growing consciousness, was more in the divine, i.e., unconscious realm, than the corresponding hero of the much later Greek myth. Some historical explanations exist, but to my mind none of them are quite satisfactory. Still, I would like to mention one, for it throws some important sidelights on our subject. Georges Contenau, the French translator of the Gilgamesh Epic, mentions in his elaborate, and from an historical point of view most valuable, commentary, the connection with Gilgamesh's ancestry. In a Sumerian legendary list of kings (who mostly ruled for thousands of years) which separates the dynasties into those before and after the deluge, Gilgamesh is listed as the fifth king of Uruk after the flood. In this list it says:

> *The divine Lugalbanda, a shepherd, ruled 1200 years.*
> *The divine Dumuzi* [=Tammuz], *a fisher, who was born in Eridu, ruled 100 years. Gilgamesh, whose father was a*

Lil-la, *a priest of Kullab* [= the holy quarters of Uruk]
reigned 126 years. Ur-Nungal, Gilgamesh's son,
reigned 30 years.... etc.

(Contenau, p. 205f)

The times get shorter after Gilgamesh, and Contenau
remarks that the dynasty of Uruk had its place shortly before
one reaches historical grounds. He, with many others, holds
that Dumuzi (Tammuz) and Gilgamesh were real kings who
were subsequently deified. In our connection this is of sec-
ondary importance, for legends, which arise around historical persons, and which contain more or less mythological
features, always originated in the unconscious of later times,
or even already during their own lifetimes. From the description of Gilgamesh which we have already read, there
can be no doubt that we have to do with a truly mythical
figure, as will be still more evident in the whole structure of
the epic.

2. A Dark Origin

But from the psychological point of view, this list is interesting on account of this *Lil-la*, whose son he is said to be.
For according to Contenau, *Lil-la* means "imbecile," "half-
crazy." There is a poem translated into French by F. Thureau-
Dangin, about a god *Lillu*, who had such a character, re-
tracing his sad destiny. From his paternal, human side,
Gilgamesh is here shown to have a dark, imperfect heritage,
which would not be meaningless in view of his not infrequent
emotional outbreaks, which we will soon meet – at the very
beginning of the epic. Moreover, his name, which sometimes is also written *Gi-bil-agamesh,* and also *Gish-bil-ga-mesh,*
contains the name of the Sumerian god of fire, *Gibil.* Contenau refers to the biblical Samson, who had moments of
being overwhelmed by emotions, and likewise the Greek
Heracles, and he sees a general influence of the Gilgamesh

Epic on the stories of both these heroes. He does not however-
er go as far as the earlier Peter Jensen, who wrote a volumi-
nous work on the Gilgamesh Epic in world literature, and
was so fascinated by the epic that he sees in it the pattern of
all other myths and sagas, like Faust who sees Helen in every
woman.

If we want to give some weight to this strange mythological parallel, rather than being a literary influence, we see it
as being a typical characteristic of the fate of the hero,
revealing the perils of the soul of early consciousness, which
is always in danger of being overwhelmed by unconscious
impulses. Contenau, however, thinks that the term *Lil-la* has
more likely to be linked with the term *Lil-lû,* who is a demon.
His feminine counterpart, *Ardat-lil-li,* is a succubus, dangerous to men. Correspondingly *Lil-lû* is an incubus, who would
have united with Gilgamesh's mother, the goddess Nin-Sun,
a priestess of the sun-god Shamash, without the knowledge
of her husband, the divine Lugalbanda. So Gilgamesh would
be the offspring of a goddess and a demon. There are other
such examples, as in the legend of Lilith, a female demon
who kills children at night. Until the late middle ages, among
Jewish circles, there were still amulets worn by women about
to give birth, so that Lilith could not come and harm their
children. Lilith appears only once in the Old Testament, in
Isaiah 34:14, among the desert demons. (The Hebrew Lilith
is rendered differently in the various English translations: as
screech owl in the King James version, night-hag in the
Revised Standard version, and as night-monster in that of
the Jewish Publication Society.) In Babylon she is *Lil-li-tû,* a
nightmare, one could say, turned especially against children
and mothers, but also a succubus in men's dreams and
phantasies. She is really the negative mother, killing the
children. There is a post-Biblical legend about Lilith as the
first wife of Adam, and that they produced demons as offspring, and only then was Eve created. Here it is reversed –
Adam was the man, and Lilith was the feminine demon, but
if we accept Contenau's reasoning, Gilgamesh was the off-

spring of a goddess and a male demon. The demonic realm does not belong to the gods; it's something between the gods and man.

Also this conception of the name of Gilgamesh's father would point psychologically to a dark origin, which we should keep in mind. But Contenau's conclusion that this explains the description of Gilgamesh as being 2/3 divine and 1/3 human does not seem quite to explain this specific proportion, although it throws a significant light on the double nature of the hero.

I should only like to add Hugo Gressmann's attempt at an explanation. In his comment to Ungnad's translation he states that the prophet Elisha acquires two-thirds of Elijah's spirit, which probably goes back to the custom that the eldest son, who was the favorite son, got two-thirds of the inheritance. Thus it might be that the two-thirds god Gilgamesh was the darling of the gods, which would fit in very well

Picture 1: Lilith

with the archetype of the hero. This custom of the favorite son receiving two-thirds of the inheritance, has, however, not been proven in the case of Babylon, although this does not mean that it did not exist there, since the texts which have been found to date are still a chance collection.

3. His Tyrannical Drivenness

Immediately following this hymn-like laudatory description of the hero, we are transported into the mythical drama itself. Gilgamesh is presented as a king who oppresses his people. He harnesses their entire strength to build up the walls of Uruk and of Eanna, the dwelling of Ishtar, his achievement so intently dwelt upon in the introduction.

> *The men of Uruk fume in their chambers:*
> *"Gilgamesh leaves no son to his father;*
> *Day and night his outrageousness continues unrestrained.*
> *Yet Gilgamesh is the shepherd of Uruk, the enclosure.*
> *He is our shepherd, strong, handsome, and wise.*
> *Gilgamesh leaves no virgin to her lover,*
> *The daughter of a warrior, the chosen of a noble!"*
> *Their lament the gods heard over and over again.*
>
> (Tabl. I, col. ii, lines 11-18, Heidel p. 18)

In this mythological "dream" we understood the hero as representing a kind of ego, as an intuitive anticipation of a further development of the ego as the carrier of increasing consciousness. With this in mind, what could the people stand for, and what psychological situation is indicated in this relationship between the king and his people? The people, as the indiscriminate many, against the outstanding one, the king, symbolize the unconscious, the instinctive forces, which are here shown in a deplorable state of suppression by an ego possessed by an ambitious self-assigned task. However, this image is too one-sided if we do not consider the nature of this task: the building of the city wall, and the temple as the spiritual center of the city. True, the people are oppressed, but we must take into consideration that it is by a *cultural* task. So we can see a general psychological truth shimmering through this appalling image. Every cultural achievement is connected with some sacrifice of nature. Let me remind you of the general idea of alchemy that the work of creating the gold or the *corpus incorructible,* the incorruptible body, is an *opus contra naturam,* a work against nature. This does not contradict the idea that this very spirit, which forces man to suppress nature for certain developmental tasks, is *also* nature. This is what is behind primitive initiation rites in which they torture their own nature, as Jung makes clear in his *Symbols of Transformation,* which gives a wonderful survey of the development of human consciousness. There is an urge in nature to overcome itself. Jung often quotes the alchemist Democritus who said: "Nature rejoices in nature, nature subdues nature, nature rules over nature." Just as with modern man there is no individual task in the process of individuation which is not connected with some sacrifice of an old attitude, no rebirth without a death, so to speak, so there is no cultural task in the development of human consciousness mirrored in a myth which does not require a sacrifice of nature. But if this goes too far, as it seems to do here, nature becomes rebellious. The instinctive forces no longer cooperate helpfully in the cultural task, but stand up against it. Gilgamesh and his people here become a symbol of a psychic situation in which a split occurs between the conscious attitude and the instinctive forces.

The next step is the lament of the oppressed people, for the tyranny went too far. The text says that Gilgamesh did not leave any son to his father, nor any virgin to her lover.*

* Editor's note: This last phrase is a reconstruction of a marred text, and Speiser surmises "the maid to her *mother,*" and so too Tigay. Some commentators see here a reference to the *jus primae noctis,* the ancient right of the king or feudal lord to have the bride for the first night after the nuptials; and to besting the young men in single combat or in athletic
...

He broke into the lives of his people by using them for his task in a tyrannical way. This presents an image of an ego so possessed by a particular goal that it overrides instinctive nature. You can do this quite individually with yourself, with a resulting heart attack, or one of the well known psychosomatic illnesses. Being driven, one overdoes things not only psychologically, but also physically. It is usually the body, our age-old instinctive remnant, which reminds us if we are no longer in tune with it. In our story, the people cry to the gods, an image, as remarked, of a split between the ego and the instinctive forces.

4. The Creation of Enkidu

But it does not come to a fatal split. The fact is that myths, in most cases, indicate a positive possibility for the solution of a conflict, i.e., the possibility of integration, and not the negative one of disintegration. This is to be seen in our myth by the fact that when the people cry to the gods, the gods answer their petition. In our approach to understanding the myth, like a dream, on the subjective level, we could say that the gods correspond to the Self, which, although including both, is the wholeness superordinate to ego and instinct. The gods respond to the cry of the people with an ingenious idea, as would be expected of gods; to create a being, Enkidu, to be a companion to Gilgamesh. Naturally we need not understand the idea as a rationally conscious consideration, but as an immediate knowledge appropriate to the psychological situation, namely to create somebody whose pull is strong enough to get him out of the possession of this wall-building business. It must be something which has an equal

contests. Some support for this view is adduced from other ancient texts, but the epic does not make this very clear. If it were so, it would simply add to the image of Gilgamesh the quality of one possessed by overwhelming drives. But the consensus is that he forced them to labor on the building of the wall, the glory of which is a prominent part of the introductory praise for his achievements.

or greater attraction, to really pull someone out of such a possession. We will see later why Enkidu did have this quality, that he was a counterpart of Gilgamesh, belonging to him. The sky god Anu commands Aruru, a mother goddess, to create "an equal" to Gilgamesh with whom he can strive, so that he may release the population of Uruk. It is noteworthy in this connection that Aruru appears in other Babylonian texts as an aspect of Ishtar, sharing the same epithet: Belit ile = mistress of the gods. The text goes on:

> *When Aruru heard this, she conceived in her heart an image of Anu;*
> *Aruru washed her hands, pinched off clay,*
> > *and threw it on the steppe:*
> *... valiant Enkidu she created, the offspring.... of Ninurta*
> > [the god of war].
> *His whole body is covered with hair, the hair of his head is like*
> > *that of a woman;*
> *The locks of the hair of his head sprout like grain.*
> *He knows nothing about people or land, he is clad in a garb like*
> > *Sumuqan* [god of cattle and plants].
> *With the gazelles he eats grass;*
> *With the game he presses on to the drinking place;*
> *With the animals his heart delights at the water.*
> > (col. ii, lines 33-41, Heidel p. 18f)

So Enkidu has been created. He is described as the primeval man, the animal-like man. He is the divine chthonic counterpart of Gilgamesh. One might be tempted to see in Enkidu merely the shadow of Gilgamesh, but he seems to me to reach back beyond the shadow, into the divine animal. Now what does it mean when this animal-like, primeval man, who in his essence is really more primitive than Gilgamesh, is created *after* him? It seems to me to point to the fact that a content of the unconscious which has been there a long time, or even eternally, now, appearing in consciousness for the first time, is regarded as if it had just come into existence. Enkidu is a *new* image of the primeval man *corresponding* to the level of consciousness which is represented by Gilgamesh.

Concerning the detail that Aruru creates Enkidu out of clay: there are Old Testament and Egyptian parallels, as well as examples from Greece and many primitive cultures. Besides the familiar story of the creation of Adam (Gen.2:7), I will mention only Job 10:8f where Job speaking to God says: "Thy hands have framed me and fashioned me.... Remember, I beseech Thee, that Thou hast fashioned me as clay," and again in chapter 33:6 where Elihu, one of Job's friends, says: "I also am formed out of the clay." In Egyptian mythology the god Chnum creates the human being on a potter's wheel.

Aruru creates Enkidu *in the image of Anu*, the god of heaven. Here the divine character of Enkidu is again apparent. This passage may be the prototype of the Biblical conception in Genesis that God created man in His image. It is strange that this *chthonic* primeval man should be created in the image of the heavenly god. There is a really wide span between this animal-man and the remote god of heaven, which, I feel, indicates the great range of human development, reaching from the animal to the god. "Ye are gods," it says in Psalm 82:6, "And all of you sons of the Most High." But it also shows a hidden Luciferian quality in Enkidu which will be confirmed in two of Gilgamesh's dreams. Enkidu falls, so to speak, from heaven as the dark one, in order to change again into, or with, the higher human being, Gilgamesh, back to his primeval "heavenly" light-bringing nature.

Enkidu, who lives with the animals on the steppe and eats and drinks with them, is discovered by a hunter, who is struck dumb with fright when he sees this Pan-like figure. He runs home and tells his father of his experience, of meeting this fearful figure, "the strongest on the steppe," who tears up his traps and does not allow him to catch the game. The father advises him to tell Gilgamesh his story, and to ask him for a hierodule, that is, a temple prostitute, an Ishtar priestess, to accompany him and to seduce Enkidu, which Gilgamesh does. The hunter comes from Gilgamesh's world. It is his task to hunt animals in the wild. Psychologically this could mean the intuitive function, which discovers a new content in the unconscious, in the wilderness, a content which is meant to come into Gilgamesh's field of consciousness. But the hunter cannot bring them together. He can only bring the news of Enkidu's existence. It requires an anima-figure as a mediatrix; the hierodule, a courtesan, as Heidel calls her in his translation. The literal meaning of the word is sacred servant, i.e., of a god or goddess, more often the latter.

5. The Hierodule: Prostitute or Priestess?

In order better to understand what follows I will give you some information about the role and position of the hierodules. Hierodule means, literally, 'servant of the god.' There were hierodules not only in Babylon, for evidence of their presence has been found also in Cyprus, Greece, North Africa, and even as far as Sicily. They were connected with the worship of a deity, and their functions included sexual rites. They had a very important position in the temples of Babylon, and in the ancient Near East in general. The archaic attitude which created this holy prostitution is difficult for many modern people to grasp, particularly if they are not conscious of their complexes. The hierodule sent with the hunter is called a *harimtu*, a woman who was *herem*, which means 'under the ban of the godhead,' i.e., dedicated to the deity, in our case, to Ishtar, whence she was called *harimtu*. The word *herem* also exists in the related Semitic language Hebrew, though with an interestingly drastic change of meaning. Originally, as we have said, it meant consecrated to, dedicated to, hence belonging to a deity, whence it most likely took on the meaning of being banned to a mortal. So it came to mean a ban. Thus a person put into *herem* is under a ban, and may not be communicated with. In effect, he is excommunicated, no longer a member of the community, as happened to Spinoza because of what were considered his heretical ideas.

There are various names for, and different classes of, hierodules, as we learn from the Code of Hammurabi. I will mention some of the terms used, which are psychologically interesting. (Some, like *harimtu,* are Semitic, but many are Sumerian, for hierodulism went back into Sumerian times. Not only that, but when the cuneiform script was adapted to Semitic, the Sumerian language was kept for a longer time as a cult and legal language.) For instance *Nin-an,* 'woman of god'; *Sal-zikrum,* 'vowed woman,' or possibly 'man-woman,' if one understands *zikrum* as coming from another root, namely *zakarû* = masculine. *Sal-nu-gig,* which is rendered in bilingual texts, i.e., Sumerian and Akkadian, as *qadishtû,* that is, the sacred one, the one who is singled out or chosen. The *qadishtû,* in Hebrew, *qedeshah,* appears in several passages in the Bible, for instance in Genesis 38:21 in the story of Judah and Tamar, although there, as elsewhere in the Bible it is translated as 'harlot' and equated with *zonah,* 'prostitute.' In prophetic times the institution of *qedishuth* or hierodulism, was severely prohibited. Another interesting name is *Sal-nu-bar,* which is defined as *Zer-mashitû,* which means 'sperm purifying' or 'sperm forgetting.' This name may have to do with the belief, which is disputed, that hierodules, though permitted to marry, were forbidden to have children. When they married they brought another woman with them to bear children. It sometimes happened that they had children nevertheless, but they kept it secret and often cast them out. Thus one high-born hierodule, the mother of King Sargon of Akkad, was said to have abandoned her son in a little basket – a famous parallel and probably the prototype of the story of Moses – but a gardener found him and brought him up, and he became king and the lover of Ishtar.

The different names designate different classes of hierodule; there was a hierarchy among them. The Code of Hammurabi provides that in cases where the father did not leave a will, the *Sal-zikrû* inherited the same amount as her brothers, whereas the *qadishtû* and *Zer-mashitû* received only a third of a brother's portion, indicating that they belonged to a lower class of hierodules. We have a description of the hierodules in Herodotus:

"The Babylonians have one most shameful custom. Every woman born in the country must once in her life go and sit down in the precinct of Venus, and there consort with a stranger" (Ishtar, like the Roman Venus, was also a love goddess. His 'precinct of Venus' refers to the temple of Ishtar.) "Many of wealthier sort, who are too proud to mix with the others, drive in covered carriages to the precinct, followed by a goodly train of attendants, and there take their station. But the larger number seat themselves within the holy enclosure with wreaths of string about their heads – and here there is always a great crowd, some coming and others going; lines of cord mark out paths in all directions among the women, and the strangers pass along them to make their choice. A woman who has once taken her seat is not allowed to return home till one of the strangers throws a silver coin into her lap, and takes her with him beyond the holy ground. When he throws the coin he says these words: 'The goddess Mylitta prosper thee.' " (Mylitta is the Assyrian name of the love goddess.) "The silver coin may be of any size. It cannot be refused, for that is forbidden by law, since once thrown it is sacred." (Here you can see the ritual aspect of it. The whole is a ritual.) "The woman goes with the first man who throws her money, and rejects no one. When she has gone with him, and so satisfied the goddess, she returns home, and from that time no gift however great will prevail with her. Such of the women who are tall and beautiful are soon released, but others who are ugly have to stay a long time before they can fulfil the law. Some have waited three or four years in the precinct. A custom very much like this is found also in certain parts of the island of Cyprus."

(Herodotus Bk. 1, Ch. 199)

Now there is a large literature about the reliability of this source. Herodotus, who lived in the fifth century B.C.E., traveled a great deal in Babylon and elsewhere. According

to his description, quite apart from the consecrated hierodules, it seems to have been the custom that every woman,
probably before her marriage, should sleep once with a
stranger in the temple. Meissner, one of the earlier distin-
guished German Assyriologists, who wrote extensively on
the religion of Babylon and Assyria, and also other scholars,
think this is a misunderstanding on the part of Herodotus,
and that what he really described were the hierodules. But
others agree with Herodotus. It would lead us too far to go
into all the arguments pro and con. In any case, Herodotus,
as you have heard, considered this institution a most
shameful one. And most of the modern comments share
this moral judgment. This comes partly from a deep misunderstanding, due, as I think we may now say, to a projection
of current views onto this highly archaic time. We just cannot
judge other religions from our frame of mind. Unfortunately
it is still much too often done. A Sumerian scholar who gave
a lecture at the University of Zurich, and to whom I am
indebted for a good deal of factual knowledge, was one who
just took the whole hierodule problem as a clear matter of
prostitution. He would say: "Well, there were the young lads
who would say to their girls 'See you tonight in the temple.'"
That was really taking away all the numinosity which adheres
to a ritual. I have heard lectures on Buddhism where the
measuring stick was Christianity, which can lead to certain
results, but certainly not to a phenomenological understanding of something which is strange. This does not mean
that one cannot compare, once one has gotten the atmosphere of a foreign religion. Naturally one can compare. But
if you use one religion to understand another, you just get
out what you put in, and you do not do justice to the
phenomenon. Of course we have our limits. We cannot
jump out of our skins. We have our prejudices, and it is best
that we be aware of them, for then we may avoid some. But,
at least as an ideal attitude, the thing to strive for is the
greatest possible objectivity – and to be aware of our feeling
reactions. We cannot avoid them, nor should we, but we

should be aware of them, and not mistake them for scientific criteria. So I think something of a projection is at work here. Certainly, for an outsider, this behavior has something very startling, and perhaps repelling, but if we go a little deeper, we might be able to understand it. We might, with the help of the archaic layers in our own soul, to which we come closer in our own inner journey, understand things which are remote in time and in feeling for us. Our own dream material can confront us with very archaic rituals and happenings. This is the reason why Jung felt himself compelled to know more about religious history – in order to understand modern dreams.

As I said, one factor in the depreciative misunderstanding could be the projection of conscious or unconscious views and emotional likes or dislikes. But people caught in such views miss the aspect of sacred mystery in this kind of prostitution. We must not forget that the hierodules were *priestesses*. Jung writes in this connection in an English seminar (Winter '31, p. 257f):

> "To the primitive mind things have an entirely different value. What we call spiritual or material are to them not separated ..... the body is soul and the soul is body; there is no difference. What one does with the body may be highly spiritual, and what one does with the mind may be highly material."

Now I must add something to help explain this negative view of the hierodule. It is not only projection, but a certain unclarity in the facts themselves. The situation in itself is not so clear-cut because of the manifold, ambivalent, oscillating character of Ishtar herself, and consequently also in her servants, the hierodules. One cannot make such a neat discrimination between ordinary prostitutes and hierodules, although it was meant to be clearly differentiated. It is again Georges Contenau who mentions some most interesting details about this goddess and her cult in Uruk. Ishtar lives in Uruk in her temple Eanna (= the house of heaven), just as

Gilgamesh lives in his royal palace. She is surrounded by her court of priestesses, the hierodules, which Heidel translates as 'courtesan,' Speiser as 'harlot-lass,' which is somewhat belittling and making nice at the same time, but not in the spirit of the office, and Thompson as 'courtesan-girl, a hetaera.' The term is difficult to translate so as to differentiate it from the ordinary prostitute. Although in the later Assyrian epoch Ishtar was predominantly a warrior goddess, here, in the south, in Uruk, she is mainly the goddess of fertility as well as a nourishing mother goddess. Thus she reminds King Assurbanipal, in a dream, that she had been nourishing him with her milk. The protocols of the 3rd and 2nd millennia talk of the kings as the husbands of Ishtar, or of a goddess synonymous to her.

6. *Kalili* of the Windows

She had become, as we will see later, more and more the central goddess figure, integrating all feminine aspects represented by the different goddesses. There are many different goddesses, and there is not a one, including those appearing in the Gilgamesh Epic, whose name cannot be shown to be synonymous with Ishtar, on the basis of known texts. She is a kind of total symbol of feminine aspects at this early time. Now among those goddesses who were, as it were, absorbed into this great goddess figure, is a very particular one called *Kalili Sha apâti*, that is, '*Kalili* of the windows.' This is an Ishtar looking out of the window and calling men, and bringing them misfortune. There is a prayer which reads:

> *You are* Kalili *who leans out of the window,*
> *Who listens to the words which the men utter,*
> *Who is the cause for the young girl to desert her bed.*
> *You have caused my loss.*
> *You have placed your feet on me, O great Ishtar.*

*Picture 2: A Lady at her Window,
perhaps "Kalili of the windows"?*

This shows the other aspect of Ishtar. She is thus the instigator of anima projections in men, leading them down the garden path, and also of animus possession in women, making the young girl desert her bed. Another of her epithets is *Kalili Mu-shirtû,* '*Kalili* who bends down,' 'the queen of the window,' and *Mu-shirtû* became a synonym for a common prostitute. So she was Ishtar, the patroness of brothels. As Contineau paraphrases it: *"La patronne des lieux de plaisir et de celles qui le dispensent,"* the patroness of places of pleasure and of those who dispense it. The cuneiform sign for one of her names is the image of a reed curtain in a brothel. There was a legal and clear distinction between the common prostitute and the hierodule, who was protected from slander by the same law which guarded the good name of married women. Already in the figure of Ishtar herself, who embraces both aspects, namely the sacred aspect of the *hieros gamos* and the sacred prostitution as a symbol of it on the one hand, and the practice of common prostitution on the other, there lies a temptation to confuse them, or let us say, a difficulty to always clearly differentiate them. Some of the aforementioned terms seem to have been used for both, and that is also confusing. *Harimtu* is obviously a sacred prostitute, but later you find it also used for ordinary prostitutes. Contenau mentions a Babylonian proverb which says "Never marry a prostitute (*Zer-mashitû* is the word in the text, 'the one who forgets the sperms') who gives herself to everybody; in your misery she will not support you; in your law-suit she will calumniate you; she has no respect nor submission. Surely she destroys a house, etc. The one who marries her will not prosper." And here *Zer-mashitû* is used for an ordinary prostitute. But still the law forbid the hierodule to open a tavern on pain of death. They were reminded: "Remember to avoid taverns!" The mere fact of the existence of such laws and sayings indicates that the line between the two was not always observed, and hierodules obviously could submit to the temptation. Seen from the outside, the two forms of prostitution might not always have been easy to distinguish. But the deeper meaning of the sacred prostitution was as a symbol of the *hieros gamos*, the holy union of god and goddess. We can see it as an example of sympathetic magic. To fulfill the same act was to participate in its realization in the divine realm.

I was asked if there were any reports as to what it did to the hierodule in her own development. This is a question which invites projections. They, the hierodules, were instruments. They were, or should have been, in a *participation mystique* with the goddess or with the god, and we cannot assume the same level of conscious awareness which we, presumably, have. We have descriptions of the feelings of Gilgamesh, of Enkidu, of the gods, but not of the hierodule. We can only guess her character from how she acts and what she does, when she appears, and when she disappears. What we can do at best is to get a little deeper into the spirit of a very removed time – removed on the one hand, yet not on the other, since these archaic layers still exist in our own psyche. So there exists the possibility that we can better understand former times, and that former times can help us better to understand ourselves. We will find the motif of the *hieros gamos* later in our epic, and will deal more with it on that occasion. Here we are still concerned with our hierodule who is to help bring Enkidu to Uruk.

7. The Seduction of Enkidu

There cannot be any doubt about her role being a spiritual one. It begins by her luring him away from his total submersion in the animal world. That was the intent with which Gilgamesh sent the hierodule back with the hunter, saying:

> "Go, my hunter, take with thee a courtesan, a prostitute,
> And when he waters the game at the drinking-place,
> She shall pull off her clothing, laying bare her ripeness.

> *When he sees her, he will approach her,*
> *But then his game, which grew up on his steppe, will change its*
> *attitude toward him.* "
> (col. iii, lines 41-45, Heidel p. 21 and Speiser)

Speiser here has that they will reject him, but in a footnote to 'reject,' has "Lit. regard as stranger, deny," which we will soon discuss. And so it happens. (Here I will use Speiser's translation, for, sadly amusing, Heidel, as he says in his preface, has had "the more objectionable passages" translated into Latin! So, for instance, the third line in the above passage, which is from Speiser.) When Enkidu and the animals come to the watering-place:

> *The lass freed her breasts, bared her bosom,*
> *and he possessed her ripeness.*
> *She was not bashful as she welcomed his ardor*
> *She laid aside her cloth and he rested upon her.*
> *She treated him, the savage, to a woman's task,*
> *As his love was drawn unto her.*
> *For six days and seven nights Enkidu comes forth,*
> *mating with the lass.*
> *After he had had his fill of her charms,*
> *He set his face toward his wild beasts.*
> *On seeing him, Enkidu, the gazelles ran off,*
> *The wild beasts of the steppe drew away from his body.*
> (col. iv, lines 16-25, Speiser, ANET, p. 75)

That he spent six days and seven nights with her may well be related to the fact that the seventh day had a special significance for the Babylonians. Our Sabbath is most probably derived from the Akkadian *sabattu,* though with a total reversal of meaning. They had a lunar calender, and the month was divided into quarters. To this day our almanacs note the moon's quarters. For them, the 7th, 14th, 21st and 28th days were unlucky if not evil days, involving a number of tabus, and sacrifices to various gods were offered on them. The day began in the evening, so six days and seven nights would be a full period, to be followed by a sacrifice, each week to different gods, including Ishtar and Shamash, the sun-god, among others. We may surmise, from what followed Enkidu's week with the hierodule, that a sacrifice, however unwitting, was required of him, as is all too clear in the text. The animals reject him, deny him, they regard him as a stranger, as we noted above. He has lost, sacrificed, his identification with them, however unintentionally. This is a terrible shock to him.

> *Enkidu tried to hasten after them,*
> > *but his body was as if it were bound.*
> *His knees failed him who tried to run after his game.*
> > (lines 26-27, Heidel p. 22)

This running away of the animals – how should we understand this? He falls into the lures of the hierodule, so the plot works perfectly, and then he wants to leave her, to go back, and the animals run away from him.

REMARK: He's had intercourse with a human being, and therefore, from the animal's standpoint, he's no longer one of them.

8. The Broken *Participation Mystique*

Yes, he is changed. We just have to define a little bit more, why, and also, how does he realize it? That is very important. He realizes it not by the experience itself, but by the reaction. And that is very interesting psychologically. That can happen to us today too. One can be unaware of something happening to oneself until one gets a reaction, a mirror. And it is so important that we get reactions, because living in a splendid isolation we can have wonderful ideas about ourselves. Or even terribly negative ideas. We do not really know ourselves without being confronted. It is because the animals run away from him that Enkidu realizes that something has happened. He still does not understand it. He is just terribly shocked. And from the very fact that he is so shocked you see that it is the last thing he expected. The animals run away from him, as was remarked, because he is no longer one of them; the *participation mystique* with the animals is broken by his having been with the hierodule. He is, from the animal point of view, as it were, contaminated by another realm of life, the human realm.

Incidentally, although I am not familiar with the field, I have heard that there are some animals who will not accept their young if they have been touched by man. I remember a neighbor who, during the war, raised some rabbits in his garden. The children would take the young ones out of the cage and play with them, and then the mother rabbit ignored them, would not have anything to do with them. As though animals can have this strange instinctive feeling that 'this one does not belong to us any more.' And so here, the animals run away. It is a marvelous picture – you get at the real happening – something *happened* to Enkidu alienating him from his animal nature, although he is still the same Enkidu. But this knowledge is not yet available to him; he does not feel or know it yet. He is not reflective. He is much too primitive for that. The real things must first happen. If we know about them beforehand, and so think we already have them, we might already be wrong, so it is very good to meet reactions, as in this case. But we must be careful now not to think that this already made him human. It did not. He is still the same animal man. But to be exact we must say that he was not separated from his animal nature, but from his *participation mystique*, from his identification with his animal nature. Before he was nothing but animal nature. If we were to be altogether cut off from our animal nature, we would lose our instincts. We are neither all animal nor all spirit. The question is whether we are identical with only one side of us. For Enkidu, that spell, that magic unity, is broken – for good. Looking at Enkidu as a figure in himself, we will see that he goes through several experiences where something is broken, for his feeling, in a tragic way, for 'his knees failed him who tried to run after his game.' It was a catastrophe for him, that he could not return to his animals. There will be several such instances where he is stricken with grief. We will soon meet a depression he has because something is gone forever.

I think that was a beautiful image for a simple psychological truth: once we know something, a former state of not knowing is gone forever. We may fool ourselves about it, but not for long. That is the meaning, for instance, of the flaming sword in the paradise story, which prevented Adam and Eve from returning to the garden of Eden after they were driven out. The sword, like other sharp instruments, which can cut something in two, take it apart, analyze it, is a symbol of discrimination, a quality of consciousness. I understand the flaming sword as that knowledge which they gained by eating of the fruit of the tree of the knowledge of good and evil, of the opposites. It is that very knowledge which prevents their return to the paradise of naive ignorance. I think it is a bliss to be enlightened, but it is also the sacrifice of the former state of not knowing. Increasing knowledge is paid for by painful experiences, but maybe we would not learn otherwise. Jung once said that the deep meaning of the very cruel initiation rites among primitives is that without pain there is no learning. After having been initiated, the youngster can say: "here, where I have this burn or scar, he said such and such to me," referring to the sacred history of the tribe which was told during the painful initiation. The story was literally burned into their flesh. And I think that even without a formal ritual, that often the *real* things we have to know are also burned into us, because we do not learn otherwise. So Enkidu has to go through this terrible shock, that his animals run away, that he is no longer one of them. We can say that through his experience with the hierodule, Enkidu is no longer identical with his animal nature.

9. The Education of Enkidu; Being Meant

But he had intelligence, wide was his understanding.
He returned and sat at the feet of the courtesan,
Looking at the courtesan,
And his ears listening as the courtesan speaks.

(lines 29-32, Heidel p. 22)

Not having any other way out, it would seem, he goes back to the hierodule. But now comes something different. What happened? It is another phase. If Enkidu is changed the change must show when he comes back to the hierodule. What is changed? It is no longer the sexual instinct which is in the foreground, but intelligence, understanding. He is sitting at her feet, looking at her, listening to her. Through this shock he has become open to the real purpose behind the hierodule's coming; namely to bring him closer to the human, to bring him to Uruk. The deeper meaning of her seduction was not to bring him back as a chained bear to be shown around. That was not the purpose. For that the hunter had no need of the hierodule. He could have taken ten men from Uruk. The deeper meaning is leading Enkidu, a symbol of the animal man, into civilization. We will have ample proof of it as we go on. The text is very beautiful in giving this step by step in very few words. "He had intelligence, wide was his understanding." Now he could understand, after having gotten this shock. He could realize that something happened to him by his contact with the hierodule; he became a different person. We can see that he was not immediately conscious about it, because he needed the reaction of no longer being accepted by the animals. But then he becomes conscious, the realization hits home, and his understanding opens. He goes back, "sits at the feet of the courtesan, looking at her, and his ears listening as the courtesan speaks." Which indicates what?

REMARK: Logos.

You mean as an opposite to eros? I would not go that far. Look at the image – a man sits at the feet of a woman and listens to what she has to say. I would still call it eros, although not limited to sexuality. As he sits at her feet she becomes a kind of teacher; she is a higher anima here. First she lures him into a sexual adventure, and now she wants to convey something to him. Insofar as she is telling him something, you may call it logos, but in this case I would refer to it as *logos spermatikos*, the creative logos of a woman, here teaching something to a man. Because he listens to her, sits at her feet, she opens something new to him. True, in the larger connection it has a quality of logos, of spirit, as it had in antiquity. Nowadays we seem to have lost this deeper, richer meaning of logos, understanding it only as logic. Logos has to do with spirit. She speaks now. Now he is ready to listen, through the shock he experienced. She tells the listener about Uruk, about the temple of Ishtar, about the god Anu, and about Gilgamesh, and that Gilgamesh already knows about him, Enkidu, through two dreams which his mother Ninsun interpreted. Ninsun is a priestess, a divine priestess, at the temple of Shamash. Her profile will come out more clearly later. She explained the dreams to Gilgamesh as a prediction that a strong and trustworthy friend would come into his life. With this last, Enkidu experiences something further. He hears the hierodule telling him 'you know, there is a king Gilgamesh in Uruk, and he had a couple of dreams, and they were about *you!* And you will be a strong and trustworthy friend to him.' Now if you were to have such an experience, being told that someone has dreamt that you would enter that person's life (things which happen, by the way), how would you feel about it? What does it give to Enkidu to hear this?

REMARKS: Self confidence. Worth.

Yes, but also ... I would think of something very specific – if this is so cast by the gods.

REMARK: Destiny.

Yes, it gives the quality of destiny. The other comments were not wrong, but they belong in the larger connection of destiny. That is the important experience at the bottom of many starts of the way of individuation – a feeling of destiny, of being meant. I remember the case of a young woman with a strong problem of a split between the instincts and a very developed intellect, and she was quite disturbed and neurotic. The first dream which made sense to her in her analysis brought about a big change. She suddenly realized that if she had such a dream where there is an inner somebody, a mysterious inner somebody who means her, who wants something from her, who is concerned about her, then she counts. That brought about a big change. It gave her a religious feeling of being meant, of being chosen, if you want, of being singled out. In a way, individuation is – and I need not tell you with what price it is paid – a kind of chosenness, namely to be meant, to have fate, to have destiny.

REMARK: To be elected.

Yes, that would be the same thing. I think that the underlying idea of the chosen people is this idea of being meant, experienced in this early time by a collective ego, by a people. This feeling of chosenness in the sense of being meant by fate, is found in virtually every hero myth. Sometimes there are predictions – think of Samson, Oedipus, Jesus – that somebody will come. Such dream messages are the hallmark of the individuation process in individuals. Once this experience of fate comes, of being meant, it is very obliging; you cannot live in nonchalant anonymity any longer. You are seen. If you are meant, you are seen, and if you are seen you have to see yourself and *have* to become conscious. Well, I think this, in germ, is what is happening to Enkidu. She tells him, 'Look, you are meant. There the great king of Uruk has dreamt of you, and his mother, the

goddess, has told him that this dream means your coming.'
It did not need any more to bring him to go with her, but it
also shows something very beautiful about how the hierodule
goes about dealing with Enkidu. How do you think she does
it? Therefore I hesitated at first to accept the 'logos,' although it was right.

REMARK: Maybe she told him that if he comes they could live together.

No, no, no, just not. Nothing of the kind. That we just
could not project. I am glad you brought it up, because one
could think that he is naturally attracted by her, and goes
because she wants him to come, but that would have to be
proven by the text, and this is just the interesting thing: the
hierodule is still with him for a while, but then she disappears. She is not even mentioned any more. As soon as
Enkidu meets Gilgamesh she is out of the picture. What you
suggest has also been proposed by Thompson, who just loves
to go into a whole phantasy of a romance – that Enkidu got
depressed because he lost the hierodule. But I would not
agree with him at all, because the text does not give any
evidence of that. We would miss the point if we would just
project a romance into this.

REMARK: Was not her task there to separate him from his instincts, from
this *participation mystique* ?

10. The Hierodule as Higher Eros

Yes, but just watch how she goes about it. She really is with
him on his own level. First she just sleeps with him. That is
where Enkidu is. And then he is rejected by his animals.
Then his shock and so to speak his downfall. Then she gives
him a phantasy: 'look, you are very important. And there is a
king, and he waits for you, and something new begins for
you.' She knows instinctively that his being rejected by the

animals is also a let-down, a defeat for him, and she builds
him up. Let us go into the text to see how she receives him.

> *"Wise art thou, O Enkidu, like a god art thou;*
> *Why dost thou run around with the animals on the steppe?*
> *Come, I will lead thee to Uruk, the enclosure,*
> *To the holy temple, the dwelling of Anu and Ishtar,*
> *The place where Gilgamesh is, the one perfect in strength,*
> *Who prevails over men like a wild ox."*
> *As she speaks to him, her words find favor;*
> *For he seeks a friend, one who understands his heart.*
> *Enkidu says to her, the courtesan:*
> *"Come, O prostitute, take me*
> *To the holy temple, the sacred dwelling of Anu and Ishtar,*
> *The place where Gilgamesh is, the one perfect in strength,*
> *Who prevails over men like a wild ox.*
> *I, I will summon him and will speak boldly;*
> *I will cry out in Uruk: 'I am the strongest!*
> *I, yea, I will change the order of things.*
> *He who was born on the steppe is the strongest; strength he has!'"*
>
> (col. iv, lines 34-47; col. v, lines 1-3, Heidel p. 22f)

You see, she inflates him. Suddenly he wants to meet that
fellow Gilgamesh. But what is also important is to see that
this hierodule has a higher eros. She receives him and fills
that inner hole created by the defeat. She compensates by
giving him an inflation: "you are like a god, you are wise," to
fill him with that self-esteem he needs. And it even goes
overboard: he will show Gilgamesh who is stronger. She
responds immediately to his awakened enthusiasm by glow-
ingly describing the life in Uruk, and only then reacts to
tune down his inflation:

> *"Come, let us go, that he may see thy face.*
> *I will show thee Gilgamesh, where he is I know well.*
> *Go to Uruk, the enclosure, O Enkidu,*
> *Where people array themselves in gorgeous festal attire,*

Where each day is a holiday.
....
To thee, O Enkidu, who rejoicest in life,
I will show Gilgamesh, a joyful man.
....
He has greater strength than thou.
Never does he rest by day or by night.
Enkidu, temper thine arrogance.
Gilgamesh – Shamash has conferred favor upon him,
And Anu, Enlil, and Ea have given him wide understanding."

(col. v, lines 4-...-22, Heidel p. 23)

REMARK: She even tells him about other girls in this text – that the people are wonderful to see. I mean that this is a sort of denial, that she did not say that *she* would stay with him.

Yes, yes, there you are. She just shows him, in glowing colors, the city life of Uruk. She has an impersonal role, and she plays it absolutely impersonally.

We will not go on now with his coming to Uruk, but will deal first with the dreams Gilgamesh had. The first dream, which he told to his mother Ninsun, was as follows:

"*My mother, last night I saw a dream.*
There were stars in the heavens;
As if it were the host of heaven one fell down to me.
I tried to lift it, but it was too heavy for me;
I tried to move it away, but I could not remove it.
The land of Uruk was standing around it,
The land was gathered around it;
The people pressed toward it,
The men thronged around it,
...... while my fellows kissed its feet;
I bent over it as over a woman
And put it at thy feet,
And thou thyself didst put it on a par with me."

(col. v, lines 26-38, Heidel p. 23f)

Ninsun, the mother, adopts Enkidu, as it were, as belonging to Gilgamesh, like a twin of his. She interprets the dream as follows:

> *"Thine equal is the star of heaven*
> ....
> *He is a strong companion, one who helps a friend in need;*
> *He is the strongest on the steppe; strength he has;*
> *And his strength is as strong as that of the host of heaven.*
> *That thou didst bend over him as over a woman,*
> *Means that he will never forsake thee.*
> *This is the meaning of thy dream."*
>
> (col. v, line 41 ... col. vi, lines 1-6, Heidel p. 24)

Now we will have to make our own interpretation, which is not a disrespect to the goddess Ninsun, but I think we have a need to understand it in yet a different way. Not in a contradictory way, but maybe in a fuller way. But we will do this, and also the second dream, in our next session.

II

THE PUZZLING DREAMS OF GILGAMESH

1. On Ancient Terms and Ancient Dreams

I would like to return briefly to the question of the translation of the term *hierodule* in the context of its religious significance in Babylon. In Thompson's older, poetic translation, he uses the term *Hetaira*, the Greek term which fits one aspect of the hierodule much better than harlot-lass or barmaid, which sound a little too contemporary. Hetaira fits the spiritual aspect very well, for she was very cultured and so was really a sort of spiritual anima to the man. As you know, in the beginning this was also the case with the geisha in Japan, who were also highly cultured. Because of the free sexual relationship you could, if you want, see them as prostitutes, but there was a spiritual aspect to it which brought them closer to the role of *femme inspiratrice* to the man, and this is really covered by the term hetaira. Only what is lacking is the religious connotation, which the hierodule in Babylon had. I prefer this translation, for it at least gives this cultural spiritual aspect. I was asked how hierodules were chosen. I can only repeat that these priestesses were a hierarchic class of the population, and the head or high priestess of the hierodules was usually a high born person. In one case I came across she was chosen to be such by the Babylonian king. One should bear in mind that the temples, no less than the palace, had a great influence in

Babylonian life. But so far I could not find any indication of what made one become a priest or priestess; whether it was just a profession one chose, or as in modern times it was felt as a vocation, or whether one was prone to enter this class by the status of the family, I cannot tell.

Before going into the dreams of Gilgamesh, I'd like to mention an important book titled "The Interpretation of Dreams in the Ancient Near East" by A. Leo Oppenheim, of the Oriental Institute of the University of Chicago. It appeared in the Transactions of the American Philosophical Society "for promoting useful knowledge," and it really does promote useful knowledge as far as the whole comparative literary background of dream reporting goes. It was very interesting for me to see, corroboratingly, how necessary it is to bring the Jungian understanding of dreams into this field. In his introduction he says:

> By the very nature of its subject matter, an investigation like the present is expected, rightly or wrongly, either to take cognizance of the achievements of the psychoanalytic school or schools, or to contribute in some way towards the research work on dreams based upon the approach and methods initiated by Sigmund Freud. The material which is to be presented in this book, however, does not lend itself readily to such treatment (for) a variety of reasons.... A purely psychoanalytic approach would yield here only distorted results. ... the personality of the dreaming person remains wholly beyond the reach of the investigation, and this deprives us of that essential information which the background of the individual, or better still, his utterances in other contexts impart to the psychoanalyst.
>
> (Oppenheim, p. 185)

Naturally, as he rightly concludes, if you know only a personalistic approach, these dreams are out. But here is the very place where knowledge of the archetypes and the amplification method has to come in; an awareness of the *collective* unconscious. Amplification by parallel motifs, as well as the understanding of dreams as compensations. What comes to our help in understanding the dreams we are dealing with is the factor of compensation. What kind of consciousness do such dreams compensate? That will be quite helpful. It is as I mentioned with Jensen, who had the hunch, felt the collective, general, typical character of the Gilgamesh Epic, had the intuition of archetypes but did not yet have the concept; so he projected on it as being *the* historical source of all other myths. If he would have had the concept of archetypes he could have understood that *this* is a basic mythological hero pattern which also occurs in other myths. I feel the same thing somewhat here; that one gets to a hindrance that one cannot climb over if one does not have the necessary concepts, which I feel that Jung has provided, to understand such material. It is a pity here, for Oppenheim comes very close to the Jungian concept when he writes, early in his introduction (p.184): "In dreams intermingle in many and curious ways the influences of the conceptual conditioning of the waking world.... and that fundamental inventory of dream-contents which is most likely shared in varying degrees by all humans of all periods."

Interestingly enough, among the several types of dreams he finds by his literary critical approach, is one in which the deity appears, to kings or priests, about which he writes (p. 185): "These revelation dreams always contain a message and occur, as a rule, only under critical circumstances and then as a privilege to the leader of the social group." Now that is exactly what fits the so-called 'big dreams.' When we have such archetypal dreams it is always in critical moments, and these are the dreams most prone to be remembered, even for a lifetime. That the leader of a social group has them, we know from primitives, and it is from them that Jung adopted the term 'big dream.' It was usually the medicine-man or shaman who had the significant dreams which were considered important for the sake of the tribe. I would like to remind you of the story Jung tells about an African medicine-man who told him very sadly that it was a long time since he no longer had any such dreams. Not since the

English took over, for now *they* rule over the fate of the tribe. So he does not dream any more. He is no longer in charge, and the gods do not guide him by these dreams because he has no power to steer the fate of the tribe. So what Oppenheim says here is really a general quality of archetypal dreams. And this is exactly what we have to do with in the dreams before us: they are highly archetypal dreams. Even granting that there were certain traditions of reporting dreams, and that only a certain category of very important dreams were reported, this cannot account for the very symbolism of the dreams. In his introduction Oppenheim seems to think that there is a lot of invention – for a purpose. But that cannot be proven, and from our experience with dreams we need not assume this. Regarding our dreams here, just as we said about the myth itself: where there are no associations there is another frame of reference available, which gives us the right to interpret such archetypal dreams. Nevertheless it is a very valuable book, also for an orientation from a historical point of view about dream material.

2. Two Parallel Dreams

Now to the dream. You remember the setting: Enkidu had returned from the animals and was sitting at the feet of the hierodule who told him in glowing colors of the life in Uruk, and about Gilgamesh who waits for him, having been told in a dream that he will meet Enkidu. The first dream, as you recall, told of a star falling down to him which was too heavy for him to lift or move, and the people of the city thronged around it and kissed its feet. So this something, which we will have to try to understand, fell as described. He bent over it as over a woman, put it at his mother Ninsun's feet, and she put it on a par with him. Ninsun interprets the dream to mean that he will have a companion, strong as the host of heaven, who will never forsake him. I would like to pass to the parallel and immediately following second dream, which is almost identical with the first, except for the main symbol. Here it is not a star creature, but an axe. The dream reads:

> *"My mother, I saw another dream.*
> *In Uruk, the enclosure, there lay an axe,*
> > *and they were gathered about it;*
> *The land of Uruk was standing about it,*
> *The land was gathered around it.*
> *The people pressed toward it,*
> *While I put it at thy feet,*
> *And bent over it as over a woman,*
> *And thou thyself didst put it on a par with me."*
>
> (col. vi, lines 8-15, Heidel p. 24)

This is a similar, almost equal dream, but the central symbol is different. In the Old Babylonian version there is a variation. I told you there were different fragments which sometimes fit into gaps in the Nineveh version which we mainly follow for it is the latest and fullest one. Naturally we will consider all the fragments which fill in a gap. Here it is not filling a gap, but is an addition, and a variation, in which Gilgamesh says:

> *"I looked at it and I rejoiced,*
> *Loving it and bending over it*
> *As over a woman.*
> *I took it and put it*
> *At my side."*
>
> (Tabl. II, col. i, lines 32-36, Heidel p. 27)

They are not easy dreams on account of the difficulty of really getting a picture of this central symbol. We see that both dreams, as far as the dynamics of the dreams go, express essentially the same thing. Something suddenly being there – in one dream falling from heaven – being surrounded by the whole people, in one dream kissing its feet and Gilgamesh trying to lift it, and here putting it at his side, and that he brings it to his mother, and it is taken as his par. Now sometimes we have dreams of the category of repeated dreams, and usually there are slight differences, but the main subject remains the same. Oppenheim took note of this duplication of dreams repeating the same message but with different symbols, and points out other examples in the Bible: Joseph's dreams of the sheaves and then the stars bowing to him (Gen.37:6ff), and Pharaoh's dreams of the seven kine and of the seven ears of corn (Gen.41:2ff.). Now what do we know of such dreams, and what is their conspicuous quality?

REMARK: Emphasis.

Yes, an emphasis. To deal with something. Why do you have to deal with something? Sometimes people have dreams over years, again and again, with little changes, but the main subject is the same. Why the emphasis? It is an insistence by the unconscious to bring the subject back again and again until something is realized. Often it is a childhood dream. Such dreams may be repeated even over a long stretch of years, and often such childhood dreams have a programmatic quality for a whole life. It was really an experience to see, in his seminar on childhood dreams, what Jung, not knowing the dreamer, got out of a childhood dream which someone in the class brought; what conclusions he drew about how the further life of the dreamer could likely develop. So, repeated dreams, not only from childhood, are very important dreams, as though the unconscious would knock at the door of consciousness again and again and say 'can you let me in *now*?' It is not infrequent that such dreams disappear when they are taken care of. That is not only a matter of good will. Sometimes it is a matter of whether or not one is ripe to integrate the material. Naturally a more continuous attention to the unconscious, as in analysis, can be favorable by its maturing process, for integrating such dreams. As you know, Jung sometimes mentions dreams he had which he did not understand for years, and only in a later connection did light fall on them, and there it was – and he could not know it before. I remember his once saying to me when I brought him a dream – an alchemistic dream – and he said it with visible satisfaction: "You know, I could not have understood your dream if I would not have known anything about alchemy." He was so impressed by the fact that amplificatory knowledge is very often the key to understanding a dream. Which is one of his main points – the importance of the method of amplification. You can always get something out of a dream, but if you reduce it only to a personal level you might miss the bigger message of it.

3. Stars and the Host of Heaven

So, if we have two dreams saying the same thing, with one difference, what conclusion can we draw? The *difference* must have a special meaning. We must ask 'why the two symbols?' So we will try to find a reason for some inner necessity, for the unconscious, to produce a second dream, almost the same, but with another symbol. We should not jump to conclusions, but we can assume that there must be two different aspects of the same thing, which are important compensatorily for the life situation of the dreamer. In the first dream we learned that something like 'the host of heaven' came down from heaven. It is heavy, it cannot be moved easily, and people kissed its feet. Do you have a picture of that? Can you see it? I think one cannot. It is an extraordinarily complex symbol. It comes from the stars, yet has a human form as we can gather, for people kiss its feet, and it is heavy as a stone. So we really cannot very easily fit it into any category of object. This naturally is the privilege of the dream – to bring us up against appearances which we cannot trace back to something ever seen before. It is especially complex, and we must try from the symbolic angle to understand what it could mean. Let us start with the first characteristic. It comes from the stars and is like one of the host of heaven. Does that ring a bell, the host of heaven? Think of Sunday school.

REMARK: The Christmas story.

Yes, but much earlier. The Old Testament. What is the host of heaven?

REMARK: Angels.

Angels? They are the *Benai HaElohim*, the sons of God, in the Old Testament. And you have too, the great Isaiah vision, in chapter 6, where he sees the seraphim around the Godhead, who say "Holy, holy, holy, is the Lord of hosts; The whole earth is full of His glory." The host of heaven is the idea of angels, but why host? One of the names of God in the Old Testament is *Yahweh Zeva'oth, Yahweh* (the Lord) of the host. *Zeva* is the army. So there is a category of angels who have a warrior character. They are star deities, old star deities, which, in the new religion, became a hierarchy of divine beings. For instance, the *Benai HaElohim* are really God-beings, if one understands the word *Ben* in a new way, which is generally accepted in the literature. This 'host of heaven' occurs only in connection with the *Benai HaElohim,* never with the *Malach Yahweh,* angel of the Lord, which is more the messenger aspect. If you are interested in this special problem of the host of heaven, I can refer you to my book on *Satan in the Old Testament,* where I have dealt more elaborately with the different categories of angels in the Old Testament. They very likely were polytheistic star deities which got a new connotation in the new Hebrew monotheism. The main passage in the Bible where you can see this host of heaven at work is in Judges 5:20, where the *stars* fight against Sisera. These are such star gods. Such changes are not rare. You can see it in the Hebrew God name Elohim, which is a plural form, and hints to a plurality of gods which were condensed into one God in the development from polytheism to monotheism. We will have some quite interesting glimpses of this process later on in our epic. But we must also think of another aspect of star. A star falling from heaven. Not only falling-stars. What is the symbolic meaning of star? There is still another important amplification possible. With what are stars frequently associated?

REMARKS: A special light. Hope. Destiny.

Hope? – too, but also destiny. That is a very well known connotation. Think of the old discipline of astrology, where the whole destiny of man is connected with, if not determined by, the stars. "Born under a lucky star." Our destiny is in the stars, which naturally means that what happens to man, and in what form, is connected with something "upper." And so the stars become a symbol of a personal destiny. And here you have the most famous example. Where did a star appear announcing something very great? Yes, with the birth of Jesus. There you have the star. And you also have star dreams, like that of Joseph, and also today. I would like to tell you an interesting story from my own experience: I have a nephew, now a young man, who on his 4th birthday said, very spontaneously, "Mother, is it not so that there is also a star having its 4th birthday?" No one recalled ever having told him any such thing. It was a spontaneous archetypal idea that a star is born with us. My star is born with me, and now is having his 4th birthday too. Children say the most amazing things – archetypal ideas right from the source – and I always tell young mothers to take the pains to write them down.

Now if we think of the fate symbolism of the star, which I think is relevant in our connection, we have to think of something else too; that this star-being falls from *heaven*. And what would that indicate? How does fate usually meet us? Sometimes just like this, just as sudden. Falling from heaven, which, symbolically would mean falling into consciousness from the unconscious. We could say that Enkidu is this star-like being falling down on Gilgamesh, so to speak, and then one could say that the dream is indicating that something of fateful importance is coming to meet him. But one might say, well, that is just an intuition – how can you prove it? How *can* you prove it? You have the frame of the whole epic, from which you can see that with Enkidu a new phase of fate came into Gilgamesh's life. He went with Enkidu on the heroic encounter, and being with him, and then losing him, brought him onto his journey to find immortality. So Enkidu is really a fate which fell into Gilgamesh's life, and we can see how true this is. We could say he became a turning point in Gilgamesh's fate.

There are additional features to this being, namely its heaviness, and immovability – which makes me think of a large stone. Incidentally, in most of the commentaries it is likened to a meteor. How much that is of help I do not know. But the image lends itself – it could be seen as a meteor. But why does he bring it to his mother Ninsun to be accepted? Why would it be a turning point in his fate? We cannot be satisfied merely with finding a similarity to an outer object, but only if this object would open up the meaning of the symbol, then yes. We must consider all these possibilities. What would it mean if it is a meteor? I do not think that leads us very far. But it has a stone-like quality – it is heavy. Merely symbolically, what would that indicate? It is a burden, heavy to carry. But also, I would say that putting the stress on the stone-like quality of this thing falling from heaven brings up another amplification. What is the symbolism of the stone frequently? This star-like thing, when it comes down, changes into a stone.

REMARK: Transformation.

Transformation too. I was thinking of the stone in alchemy. This naturally is much later, but we need not hesitate to inquire also into later connections in symbolism which can throw some light on the subject. We do know that alchemy has very early roots, for instance in ancient Egypt. All Self symbols already appear very early, and the lapis or stone of the alchemists is that *prima materia*, the first primal matter, which is meant to be changed, transformed into the *lapis philosophorum*, the philosopher's stone. Namely, the end product of a becoming firm, becoming stable, becoming incorruptible. Even if only as a side glimpse, I think we are permitted to see and to add as an implication, the stone-lapis character of this object which has all the earmarks of something terribly important for Gilgamesh, being put at his feet, having to be carried, and, as the course and end of the epic shows, which was really the factor of the transformation of Gilgamesh.

Another thing; we already dealt with the creation of Enkidu. With this in mind, the very fact that this object falls from heaven brings up something we already learned about him, about his creation, which was in the image of Anu, the god of heaven. We mentioned then what this implies. As you know, he is a half man, half animal creature, when found. But he is created to match Gilgamesh, to draw his libido away from the oppressed people. Being created in Anu's image endows him with a divine quality, which gives him a very large range of opposites, between the animal man and the divine creature. As I mentioned then, one could almost assume that he has a kind of potential Luciferian quality – Lucifer having fallen from heaven. In a later dream it will reveal itself more clearly. So we can just keep this in mind too. It all has a bearing in our connection in this very complex and not very visualizable image, in the context of our material. The context is very important, for the danger is always great to just intuit such things. We must be able to base our intuitions in the material. Beginners sometimes make this mistake, and then everything is everything. Naturally you do not get anywhere that way. Our intuitions are like lights shining in the dark, but we must then look to see whether what they shine on is really what we assumed it to be. I think that this star-like being, having an aspect of fate, falling from heaven – which fits Enkidu's creation story, its heaviness, its stone character, hints at a constellated content of the unconscious which breaks through into Gilgamesh's life at a certain crucial moment with the greatest impact, which puts him initially into a situation of not being able to cope with it. And now comes something. What helps him to cope with it? Think of the dream. He can not carry it, and then what happens? The people gather around it. The concentration of the people around this being which has fallen from heaven, behaving in a worshipful way, with reverence, this is what helps him to carry it. The help of the people is pictured more directly in the Old Babylonian version where Gilgamesh's description of the dream reads:

> "I tried to move it, but I could not move it.
> The land of Uruk was gathered around it,
> While the heroes kissed its feet.
> I put my forehead firmly against it,
> And they assisted me.
> I lifted it up and carried it to thee."

(Tabl. II, col. i, lines 9-14, Heidel p. 26)

4. The Helpful People

Earlier we spoke of the symbolic meaning of the people. If we take the hero as an anticipation of a developing ego consciousness, then the people are the carrying instincts. Here, in this dream, we have a compensatory factor of the first order. We spoke of Gilgamesh as an oppressing power-possessed ego, and there were the oppressed people who cried to the gods, who then created Enkidu to relieve the people and to direct Gilgamesh's libido to this new figure. And what is the attitude of the people now? Helpful! That gap seems to be closed in the dream. Here the compensatory function of the dream is beautifully shown. You must think of Gilgamesh sitting in Uruk, not yet knowing Enkidu, and having such a dream, which shows that what he really needs to get out of his possessed state is the help of his instincts. The dream is compensatory to the happenings described in the epic before. You see, *these* are our criteria, and without these psychological criteria you can not really understand the dream. An organizing literary point of view can be very helpful, but not for the understanding of the dream. I would say that the concentration of the people also symbolizes the concentration of the unconscious forces on these happenings. In it we see the unconscious libido centered around this new content. One could also say, since it is a dream of Gilgamesh, that his unconscious is prepared and ready in advance, to receive the new goal of libido, away from his outer possessedness and consequent oppression of his people. Taken on the subjective level, as an image of an inner psychological situation, the dream reflects a healing of the threatened disintegration of the personality. The unconscious forces being *helpful* to consciousness, present an image of integratedness. That is what we hope and strive for if we are in a split-off state from the unconscious – to be linked up with our inner instinctive forces and with the unconscious.

The plurality of the people stands for the unconscious qualities. The plurality in these dreams seems still to be away from consciousness. Then they concentrate on one figure, and thus come closer to consciousness. Whenever you have anonymous crowds it shows a content still far away, but *meant* to become conscious. Sometimes it reduces to two, when either content is very close to come over the threshold into consciousness. Because the same two emphasizes and makes you conscious of the character of the one. If you have two books of the same appearance, it catches the eye and you become aware of the appearance. Jung has dealt with this in one of his dream seminars where the motif of the twins comes up. Here we have the concentration of the plurality in a helpful way, and healing the breach which we saw at the beginning of the epic. This helps Gilgamesh to bring the load, which is too heavy for him, to his wise mother. Without the help of the unconscious, it *is* too heavy. You see that so often in analysis; people come and say 'I really do not know how you can help me. I know my problem, I know myself.' Naturally what they do not know is that it is their own unconscious which can help them, namely to carry them along by revealing a meaning, which alone gives them the strength to carry it. What we can foresee often ends up in a dead end. It is the unexpected help of the unconscious which opens up a new vista and gives us a glimpse of a possibility, of a turn, which we could never imagine before. So something seems too heavy to carry, unless something comes to help, which is a generally human situation. And it is usually the unconscious instinctive forces which help. In fairy tales, for instance, there is a category of the so-called helpful animals, which turn up when the hero or heroine is in a pinch with no visible way out; animals which they usually have helped earlier, and forgotten about, and here they are to help them out. Which symbolically means that if we treat our instincts right, they come to our help when we need them.

5. Homosexuality, Ancient and Current

Now what does it mean that Gilgamesh bent over this star-like object as over a woman? We observed that the star also signifies fate, that Enkidu falls, so to speak, on Gilgamesh as his fate. He must embrace this fate. It is an expression of the hero's *amor fati*, which presents itself in the image of a love-union. Also in the second dream, he "rejoiced, loving it and bending over it as over a woman." This seems to me to belong to that ancient homosexuality which created culture and consciousness in those times. If we look at homosexuality from the point of view of libido, libido investment, we should recall what Jung pointed out in his *Symbols of Transformation*. Libido as such is neutral, it is psychic energy, and can flow into different fields. It can be pulled into sexuality, but it can also be pulled into a spiritual field, for instance. Just as physical energy can be changed from one form to another – hydraulic to electric energy – so too psychic energy, by means of the symbol, can be transformed from one manifestation to another. From this point of view we can ask: what could it mean, in the creation of culture, that a whole era could have this inclination to homosexuality? It would be interesting to ask what the apparent increase in homosexuality *today* could mean? That would lead us a little far, but perhaps we can find certain conditions which could throw light on the modern problem too, even though now it has a very different setting. In the ancient matriarchal culture it seems as if the libido of men had to concentrate on *itself*, as it were, in order to get out of the mother. It is really a mother problem. The libido in the man tends to reach his own virility, and the virility is projected onto man. You see that also in our time, where very often there is a huge mother problem behind homosexuality. It usually is a problem of freeing the virility from the mother. One interesting example is that of a young homosexual I worked with who dreamed that he was in an Indian tribe, standing in the center of a large circle composed of all the men in the tribe. They were dancing around him in a ritual rhythm, coming closer and closer. That has all the feeling quality of an initiation rite. He was then well in his twenties, but in the dream he was going through a belated puberty rite which should have occurred at the age of thirteen or fourteen. The same young man once dreamed that he wanted to wake up, but someone was pressing his eyes closed so hard that it hurt. When he finally succeeded in opening his eyes he discovered that it was his mother pressing his eyes closed, i.e., not wanting him to become conscious. Homosexuality culturally had to do with matriarchy – which is a modern problem again. That is a similarity. But in those ancient times it seems to have been a cultural necessity to break away on a larger scale from the mother realm, to get the libido out of the mother. We will see that the mother problem is one of the major subjects in the first part of this epic, and that of immortality in the second part.

I think it throws light on our dream when we see this homosexual implication in the above sense as the very meaning of the dream, and not just simple homosexuality. This becomes still more clear in the dream of the axe. A humorous story relevant to this is the one Jung tells: when in America he was taken to visit an Indian tribe, and found only women and children and old men in the village. Where are all the men? they were asked. Just go on, you will find them, was the answer. Eventually they came to a place where they heard chanting, and saw all the men sitting under a cloth roof supported by poles, chanting "We are we! We are we!" So they had a ritual which lasted for three days – leaving the village to reassure themselves about who they were – that they were men! In puberty boys have this tendency – we are we – and "you won't tell *me*!" – which is absolutely necessary. Once, in a discussion of homosexuality, Jung said that in puberty such a phase is a necessity, because the influence of the mother is so overwhelming that only setting yourself apart and fighting it, and stressing your virility, maybe even in a silly way, but in some way, is really necessary. To stop being a good boy to please your mama. But if it perseveres and remains, then, naturally, it may become a neurotic phenomenon. But as you have seen in the dream I told you, the unconscious compensates by wanting to initiate this young man, saying: look here, now it is time; they all crowd around you, all these Indian braves, who have their virility. Naturally, it is a matter of fate, whether this pattern can change, or not.

6. The Axe

If what I have said sounds questionable, I think the axe dream is more confirming. Why in the second dream is the object an axe? The axe *splits* something. Like swords, or knives, the axe is usually a symbol of discriminating consciousness. The Hebrew language makes this very clear, because the word for understanding is *binah*, which comes from the word *bain*, which means ' between,' 'in between,' and the word *'lehavin,'* to understand, from the word *bain*, structurally means 'to put something in between.' Our language is full of images which explain themselves, if only we look for them. We have a very good example starting from the *Enuma elish*, the Akkadian creation myth. In it the god Marduk kills the primeval mother monster, Tiamat, with an arrow, a penetrating object. We also say we penetrate something with our thinking.

> *When Tiamat opened her mouth to devour him*
> *He drove in the Evil Wind that she close not her lips.*
> *As the fierce winds charged her belly,*
> *Her body was distended and her mouth was wide open.*
> *He released the arrow, it tore her belly,*
> *It cut through her insides, splitting the heart.*
> *Having thus subdued her, he extinguished her life.*
>
> (Tabl. IV, lines 97-103, Speiser, ANET, p. 7)

This image also occurs in the Old Testament, in Job 26:12, where it says of God: "And by His understanding (binah) He smiteth through Rahab." (Rahab is a synonym for Tiamat.) So in the Bible text the symbolic meaning of it replaces the image of the older myth, which naturally provides a very quick confirmation of our understanding of the symbol. So here it is the axe, which belongs with the symbolism of the sword, arrow, knife – all symbols of discriminating consciousness. Naturally, they can also be very destructive, and our consciousness can be destructive too. If we get too intellectual, for instance, and analyze something to death. The axe also belongs among the earliest human instruments, and in different early cultures it had a sacred meaning. As Jung has pointed out, with the axe one clears the woods, which gives the whole symbolism in a nutshell. The woods are the unconscious, and with the axe you make a clearing in the unconscious so light can fall through into the darkness. That's what the axe does. So it is a very primordial symbol of discriminating, developing consciousness. It is the necessary instrument in the deeds which create consciousness. It enables light to fall into the unconscious.

Now, to anticipate: Enkidu becomes the axe at Gilgamesh's side, which enables him to fulfill the heroic deed of the symbolic killing of the Mother; for with the axe Gilgamesh will fell the cedar tree in the forest (the mother symbolism of which will become still more evident), when, right after the dramatic happenings we will meet first, they go to kill the chthonic giant-god Humbaba. That reveals the meaning of the axe in the dream, and the coming of Enkidu. So we can say that the axe really stresses the masculine quality of Enkidu, which he must love as he would love a woman. That Enkidu stands for this quality for Gilgamesh we see in a later tablet where, in his lamentation over Enkidu's death he himself calls Enkidu an axe:

> *The hatchet at my side, the bow in my hand,*
> *The dagger in my belt....*
> (Tabl. VIII, col. ii, lines 4-5, Heidel p. 62 [1946 ed.])

Here you have three symbols which stand for consciousness. So I think we must come to the conclusion that Enkidu does *not* stand for the feminine quality, but Gilgamesh has to give to a man the love he would give a woman. That would mean that out of a cultural necessity of an archaic time, this libido has to be directed to virility. In these dreams the main problem of the Gilgamesh epic comes to light, namely, the overcoming of the mother. This can be understood on the psychological level, as wresting more consciousness from the matrix of the unconscious in the process of an expanding development of consciousness.

One could call such an archaic time the puberty of mankind, just as myths have been called the dreams of early mankind. If what was a time necessity prevails, or comes back, it can have a regressive quality, or the quality of a new development. It has to be seen whether it takes a positive development or a disintegrating one. We will find such situations, where it can go this way or that, several times in the epic. We have seen it first in the split of the psychic wholeness we understood the myth to represent, when Gilgamesh oppressed the people. If that split would have grown, it would have been a disintegration, psychologically. But as we saw, it took a good turn. The people became collaborative, concentrating, in the dream, around this new being who was to complete Gilgamesh. Enkidu is a necessary counterpart to Gilgamesh, a necessary connection of his. We can also see in Enkidu the *concentration* of the instincts – or, the people becoming one. Being connected with Enkidu, being united with him, gives Gilgamesh the strength *and* the animal wisdom, as we will see, to fulfill his heroic deed. The heroes always have the help of the gods in some way. They never do it out of their consciousness alone. Think of Odysseus, who got the miraculous herb Moly from Hermes when going to Circe, the dangerous anima, and was told to keep his sword handy, even in bed. Here you have the sword again. He had to have his wits about him, a sharp consciousness, while being with this dangerous anima figure. We will leave the dreams now. I just wanted to show what they are aiming at. They intuitively anticipate the opus ahead for Gilgamesh, what he is going to face. He had to have his total masculine virility before going on to his heroic deed.

7. Enkidu's Transition to Civilization

Let us return to the reality of Enkidu in the epic. The hierodule, as we have seen, succeeds in inducing him to go with her to Uruk.

> *He listened to her words and accepted her advice;*
> *The counsel of the woman*
> *He took to heart.*
>
> (Tabl. II, col. ii, lines 24-26, Heidel p. 28)

We saw that he opened up to her after going through the shock of being rejected by his companions, the animals, with whom he had lived in *participation mystique*. He came back to the hierodule, and now 'he took the counsel of the woman to heart.' There is no doubt that for Enkidu the hierodule plays an anima role, a higher anima. She introduces him to culture. On the way to Uruk she teaches him to eat and drink in a human way, for up till then he knew only how to suck milk from the animals. The cultural role of the anima could not be displayed more clearly and beautifully. One really can not understand certain upset comments like "shameful custom," etc., other than by assuming that the author is being caught in prejudices. Even if insisting that she is a prostitute and nothing but a prostitute, it should be clear that this would not be the usual function of a prostitute, except that she have a higher, spiritual function. So Thompson, in his translation as hetaira comes much closer to this role. The text says:

> *Enkidu ate bread*
> *Until he was sated;*
> *Of the strong drink he drank*
> *Seven goblets.*
> *His soul felt free and happy,*
> *His heart rejoiced,*
> *And his face shone.*
>
> (Tabl. II, col. iii, lines 15-21, Heidel p. 29)

You get the poetic quality very nicely, also in the translation. He anoints and dresses himself and becomes, as the text expressly says, "like a human being."

> *He anointed himself with oil,*
> *And he became like a human being.*
> *He put on a garment,*
> *And now he is like a man.*

(lines 24-27, Heidel p. 29)

What we really have here is the development of an animal man, by the hierodule, by this sacred prostitute or priestess, into the realm of civilized culture. It has been assumed, probably correctly, that the Enkidu story might originally have been a separate myth depicting the process of development from savage primeval man to civilized man, unconnected with the Gilgamesh Epic. But as we stated earlier, that does not prevent us from recognizing, nor even permit us to ignore, the role of the creative unconscious in bringing such myths together and melting them into one. For even had it been an independent narrative with Enkidu as the central figure, by connecting it with the Gilgamesh story, it makes perfect sense that they go together from then on. Just as the flood story, in a later tablet, which has another hero, Utnapishtim, is also linked up with Gilgamesh, and fits perfectly. Certain archetypal patterns, in the course of cultural development, can grow together and build a unity. I think there can be no doubt about the cultural importance of the hierodule in this epic. It comes very fully to light in what the myth describes. So the hierodule, who has no name, which is also an indication of her impersonal quality, leads Enkidu out of his animal existence into human existence and into the culture of society.

Enkidu's transition from the paradisical unconsciousness of animal life into the human world suggests comparison with another story where man is taken out of blissful unconsciousness; the paradise story of the Garden of Eden, the so-called fall of man. The pain connected with the transition is just as evident in the one as in the other, but how different is the atmosphere in these two stories!

REMARK: Enkidu is only part of a man. The other part is Gilgamesh, whereas Adam is the whole man.

Yes, Adam is the Anthropos, the symbol of the whole man, and Enkidu is the animal man. And besides, there, Adam had Eve at least. Those are other features. It is clearly a later development there. But we can pick out several traits in order to compare the two stories. What is the main difference in the atmosphere? Think of how it is described. "Enkidu ate bread until he was sated, of strong drink he drank seven goblets, his soul felt free and happy, his heart rejoiced and his face shone." What does one feel here? It has something joyful, natural, optimistic. It is an *ascent.* And in the Bible? It's a fall, the fall of man. That leads to very deep considerations. And something else: if one thinks of the whole coming into being of Enkidu; the gods created him for the very purpose of being led into this world. They completely approved of this development. What is the striking difference between this and the Biblical story? How did the fall of man happen in the paradise story? By going against God, by committing a sin. It is a *moral* problem. Here in the epic there is no moral problem whatsoever. Everything is still imbedded in nature – and that is the mother-world. Enkidu is led into civilization, but it still remains the mother-world. For civilization as *material* culture (material from *mater,* mother) still belongs to the mother-world. The Biblical conception of the *fall* of man arises from a conflict between this natural, unbroken, conflictless life in nature, in the mother, in paradise, and the moral demands of spirit.

REMARK: How would you connect that with what you said in your interpretation of the dream about fighting against the mother?

Enkidu must first be led into culture, and *then* the fight against the mother begins. You will see that Enkidu has the greatest resistances against going to fight Humbaba. He is the one who has the instinctive link, for whom it is a sacrilegious deed to go and fell the cedar. But that is just the deepest question: whether that is not a necessity. I would say that every fight with the mother in this cultural sense, presupposes a certain consciousness. The animal man cannot do it. In the Biblical story it is different because that myth mirrors a consciousness suffering from the conflict of knowing good and evil – suffering from the moral conflict. Consciousness of the moral conflict is the human feature. Animals do not have it, children do not have it, and we sometimes envy them thoroughly. At least I did. I remember as a child, we once had a maid who was a little feeble-minded. She was the happiest creature I ever met, and I know how I would envy her and think I would like to be like Mary. She had no conflict. She even had certain tones as of an animal happiness. I remember when I had to study and learn poems by heart, and so on, I thought, oh, how nice if one could be like Mary. I do not think so any longer. We will see that in Enkidu. The natural man in us is, from time to time, depressed, or wistful for the lost paradise. Therefore we have this idea of projecting the lost paradise into the future, which we do. But then it has another quality: regaining the naturalness by having gone through the conflict into which consciousness throws us. There is a very beautiful saying by a medieval mystic, Hugo de St. Victor, who said there is a stage when we first start out, in which mountains are mountains, valleys are valleys, and everything is in its place. Then comes a state when everything is no longer so; mountains are no mountains, everything is questioned. But *then* comes a state when mountains are again mountains. Everything falls in place again, but in another way, on another level, on a really conscious level.

The goal of individuation is not to become sophisticated, but in a deeper way to become natural and at one with oneself; finding the union between consciousness and the unconscious, as it is mirrored, for instance, in the *hieros gamos* of king and queen in alchemy, and in other Self symbolisms. To return to our comparison: the Biblical conception of the fall of man arises from a split with nature, a necessary one, in acquiring a consciousness of good and evil by eating of the fruit of the tree of knowledge. It is really the subject of every development of consciousness. We will find it later with Gilgamesh and Enkidu too. In the Gilgamesh Epic Enkidu's development means a giving up of the mere animal side, but it is not yet a split with nature. Only in the father world, one could say, does moral reflection begin, the real spiritual development. This comes out very clearly in another connection. In the Gilgamesh Epic, Utnapishtim, at the end, represents, so to speak, the last stage of development. He finds a life beyond this world, far away, beyond the reach of other men. Only the hero Gilgamesh finds the way to him. However, Utnapishtim is the prototype of Noah in the Bible; sometimes he is called the Babylonian Noah. It is Noah with whom God makes his first covenant, and with whom the divine plan of salvation, the spiritual history of mankind, in the Bible, only *begins*. We shall have yet other opportunities of considering these two worlds from the point of view of different phases of development.

Monotheism is an appearance, a development, which leads out of the polytheistic mother religions. And Yahweh is a God who has no mother and no wife. The masculine is very stressed, and is paid for with a high price – pushing the feminine into the background, as one can see very clearly in studying the Bible. It was, I would say, a tragic necessity, in order for consciousness to grow. Because in these mother cults, – Isis and Osiris, Ishtar and Tammuz – with all their beauty, there was always only an eternal return, the cycle of the year, the son-lover Tammuz being killed by the summer heat and revived in the spring, rejoiced over by all women. The feminine rituals are only in a kind of cycle, whilst the monotheistic religion has, as it were, a vertical line. Jung in a talk, once drew a most illuminating image, describing the mother religions as an uroboros, the circled serpent with its tail in its mouth. It always remained a circle. And then came a moment, a mysterious moment, when it let go of its tail and raised its head, and that created the vertical, which stands for the beginning of history really, in a progressive way. And then comes a development. Think of Christ, who belongs in a way to the row of dying and resurrecting young gods. But for him it became a once and forever happening, put into history. I do not want to go into the question of the historicity of Christ. I can only say that Christ's historicity is important for the myth, and that picks him out of the circle, of the eternally unchanging circle. When the serpent puts his head up is a mysterious moment, for one cannot really explain why consciousness came into being. You cannot explain it, and from a Darwinian point of view you will never get to catch the mystery of consciousness.

III

THE FATEFUL MEETING

1. The Fight at the Gate

Enkidu's approximation to the human condition seems to me to have a still further psychological meaning: he has to become similar to Gilgamesh in order to be accepted by him. The animal man as such is too far away, strange, and terrifyingly powerful. Such contents of the unconscious go through a transformation tending towards the human form in dreams and phantasies, until they can be assimilated by consciousness. Now when Enkidu enters Uruk, led by the hierodule, the people of Uruk stand round him and gaze at him and they say:

He looks like Gilgamesh ...
He is shorter in stature.
But stronger in bone.

(Tabl. II, col. v., lines 15-17, Heidel p. 31)

Thus Enkidu is shorter but stronger than Gilgamesh. He is the more chthonic, but the stronger one, the carrying instinctive force. Here, for the first time in this human form – we have just heard that he looks like Gilgamesh – we can see in him, looked at from Gilgamesh's side, a shadow figure which can be assimilated. The fact that he is a trifle shorter is also symbolically meaningful. It is important that this content does not reach beyond the consciousness which is represented by Gilgamesh, and cannot overwhelm it. Here again the myth presents the positive possibility of the way of conscious growth, of individuation, for in life there exists also the negative possibility of a shadow content being too large to be integrated by consciousness.

Now Gilgamesh and Enkidu meet, an event toward which everything so far has been leading. The circumstances under which this happens are of decisive importance. Gilgamesh is just about to enter the so-called family house in order to fulfill the *hieros gamos* with a hierodule or the goddess herself. At this very moment Enkidu places himself in his way, hinders him from entering, and fights with him. In the family house Ishhara's bed was already prepared, says the

Picture 3: Lovers embracing on bed

text. But Ishhara is also a synonym of Ishtar, and this actually in her mother aspect. So it is indirectly with Ishtar that Gilgamesh intends to fulfill the *hieros gamos,* according to the tradition of the old Babylonian kings, and in this he is hindered by Enkidu.

> *Enkidu blocked the gate*
> *With his foot,*
> *Not permitting Gilgamesh to enter.*
> *They grappled with each other,*
> *Snorting like bulls;*
> *They shattered the doorpost,*
> *That the wall shook*
>
> (Tabl. II, col. vi, lines 12-18, Heidel p. 32)

Thus Gilgamesh's libido which was concentrated on the mother, is literally drawn away by Enkidu. After this fight which Gilgamesh won, Enkidu praises him. Gilgamesh apparently decides to fight Humbaba in a missing part of the tablet, for when it is again legible, Enkidu tries unsuccessfully to dissuade him, and they become friends. An obscure because very incomplete passage follows, from which we learn that Enkidu has a depression.

> *The eyes of Enkidu filled with tears;*
> *He felt ill at heart*
> *And sighed bitterly.*
> *Yea, the eyes of Enkidu filled with tears;*
> *He felt ill at heart*
> *And sighed bitterly.*
> *Gilgamesh turned his face toward him*
> *And said to Enkidu:*
> *"My friend, why do thine eyes*
> *Fill with tears?*
> *Why dost thou feel so ill at heart*
> *And sigh so bitterly?"*
> *Enkidu opened his mouth*

And said to Gilgamesh:
"My friend,....
Have bound my sinews.
Mine arms have lost their power;
My strength has become weak."

(Tabl. III, col. ii, lines 72-89, Heidel p. 34)

Thompson assumes that it is the loss of the hierodule's love which makes him so sad, and he translates this passage with corresponding conjectures. But this seems to me to be a romance projected into the material. The text does not mention the hierodule again. After fulfilling her task of bringing Enkidu to Uruk and to Gilgamesh, she disappears, in accordance with the impersonal character of her office as priestess. To me, Enkidu's depression seems to be a reaction to his relation with Gilgamesh. By this, namely, he definitely gave up the animal paradise. The longing for the lost paradise comes up. Enkidu, the instinctive one, filled with presentiments, "fears" the sacrilegious deeds of germinating consciousness, sacrilegious towards the motherworld out of which he has just come. We shall meet again with such reactions on his part, especially before his death, when he curses the hunter and the hierodule who fetched him out of the steppe and brought him to Uruk.

Gilgamesh's answer is this: he draws Enkidu into his masculine decision to kill the giant Humbaba, and to cut down the cedar. Here the dream becomes reality. Gilgamesh accedes to his fate (think of the star dream!) through his union with Enkidu. The libido now aims at the heroic deed of overcoming the mother. It is significant that Enkidu hesitates to follow him and tries to deter him. He knows the cedar forest and its guardian Humbaba, and he describes him to Gilgamesh as follows:

"I learned it, my friend,
When I was still ranging at large over the open country
with the game.

For ten thousand double hours on every side the forest is
surrounded by ditches.
Who is it that would go down into its interior?
Huwawa – his roaring is like that of a flood-storm,
His mouth is fire,
His breath is death!
So why dost thou desire
To do this thing?
An irresistible onslaught is
The ... of Huwawa."

(Tabl. III, col. iii, lines 105-115, Heidel p. 34)

This cedar forest must be related to the realm of the mother out of which Enkidu has just come, and with which he is familiar. In the following we shall see that it is he who knows the way to the forest. Having failed to deter Gilgamesh, he leads him. That this cedar forest really has to do with the mother world is most clearly confirmed by the epic itself, for in the beginning of the fifth tablet, this forest is called the *throne-dais of Irnini,* but Irnini is synonymous with Ishtar in a hymn dedicated to her.

In the same passage of tablet five the mountain of the cedar is also called "the dwelling-place of the gods." It is the mountain of the gods. For this conception we also have several examples in the Old Testament. I should only like to mention Isaiah 14:13:

"I will ascend into heaven,
Above the stars of God
Will I exalt my throne;
And I will sit upon the mount of meeting, [meant: of the gods]
In the uttermost parts of the north."

We find a similar conception of the mountain and garden of God in Ezekiel 28, in which the "far-covering cherub ... walked up and down." This leads us to Humbaba, who also watches over the mountain of the gods, which is paradise. It

Picture 4: Humbaba

is said of him that his breath is fire. Here the Minotaur, the guardian of the labyrinth is a close parallel. As the Minotaur was killed by Theseus, so Humbaba is killed by Gilgamesh.

But this mountain of the gods has at the same time the character of the underworld. We have a picture of Humbaba where his face seems to be built up by a labyrinth of bowels. But the underworld, the realm of the dead, has also been called by the Babylonians the 'Palace of the bowels.' Here again the Greek parallel leads us further: The Minotaur is Chronos who was banished by Zeus to the underworld. He is the old father-spirit which has become negative, and is overcome by the son. The paradox that underworld and paradise are in such close connection in our text corresponds to the undiscriminated opposites of life and death in the mother. The cedar as the tree of life blossoms in the land of death – a symbol of the mother who gives and takes life. Humbaba, the intestinal man, the guardian of the motherly cedar forest, is, if we look at him in connection with Ishtar, the chthonic masculine spirit corresponding to her reign. He brings to mind Steissbart's function in Barlach's *Der Tote Tag* (The Dead Day), which in the service of the mother, destroys the son's bid to free himself from her. We shall see this aspect of Humbaba as the old spirit belonging to the motherworld and disappearing with it very clearly in other passages also.

I should like to draw your attention to a small but interesting detail from the psychological point of view. Gilgamesh is not only aware that it is his destiny to kill Humbaba. It is as if he, the hero, were also conscious of the fact that it is a *general* task which he is to fulfill, for he says that his deed will give him "a name everlasting." Most commentaries regard this statement, with some justice, it must be admitted, as indicating his intense ambition. However, as we will see, he sets out on this adventure only after several preparatory preliminaries including a direct turning to the sun god Shamash, the god of consciousness. As will become clear, Shamash is the instigator of this undertaking. An unconscious drive for a higher purpose may take the form, in consciousness, of an irresistible ambition. The hero, as a rule, always fulfills a cultural task of his time. He sets up something new with which his name remains connected.

2. *Rites d'entrée*

In what follows we have the description of how the two heroes prepare their undertaking. They have weapons cast, and one would expect them to start immediately, but there are three episodes which come in between, and which I shall call *rites d'entrée*. I have to mention them at least briefly on account of their psychological meaning. First Gilgamesh submits his plan to the elders of Uruk. They try to deter him.

> *"Thou art young, O Gilgamesh, and thy heart has carried thee away. Thou dost not know what thou proposest to do."*
>
> (Tabl. III, col. v, lines 190-191, Heidel p. 37)

And with the same words as Enkidu, they describe to him the awfulness of Humbaba and the madness of his enterprise. Gilgamesh listens to them, but he sticks to his plan, and then they bless him. Psychologically the counsel of the elders seems to me to represent the common sense, the wisdom of life in reality. Gilgamesh is not allowed to follow this common sense, and yet he had to face it. He would not have been sufficiently prepared for his fateful enterprise had he not *known*, i.e. realized, what it meant, looked at from the point of view of outer reality. He must know it, and go nevertheless. It is as though this aspect of his psyche, if we view the elders as a subjective element, would turn about when seeing his determination, when its fate character becomes clear, and change its mind. It is not expressly said so, but the sudden change in the elders after he held fast to his intention, is very impressive. They say:

"May thy tutelary god protect thee.
On the road home may he cause thee to return in safety.
To the quay of Uruk may he cause thee to return."

(lines 212-214, Heidel p. 38)

No sooner do they finish speaking, when we come to the next *rite d'entrée*, the next ritual leading to the deed itself. It is of a very different kind. He prostrates himself before Shamash, the sun god, and prays as follows:

"I go, O Shamash; to thee I raise my hands.
May it then be well with my soul.
Bring me back to the quay of Uruk
Place over me thy protection."

(lines 217-220, Heidel p. 38)

How does this prayer strike you, in view of his situation?

REMARKS: He's not depending on himself; he's depending on something greater than himself.
For one thing, the attention is not directed to the deed itself, but to his inner power, the survival of his soul.

Yes, something very important comes out. It is a very humble human prayer. He is not the big hero here. He trembles, knowing he has to do something very dangerous and great, and turning to his tutelary god or guardian angel, prays: 'Please let me come out safely.' Implied is: 'from what you cause me to do.' We will see that later. He turns to Shamash, which indicates that this is the god he is especially related to. In the polytheistic religions with their many gods, especially so in the Babylonian religion, there are many prayers to the different gods who have special qualities, to whom one turned in certain situations. But there are also gods who are the special god of a person. We can conclude from this prayer, and this is the first indication of it, that Shamash is Gilgamesh's special god. We will see later that

Ishtar also is of decisive importance to him. The relationship of Gilgamesh to Ishtar and to Shamash gives us a far-reaching insight into the whole development of this religion. But here, Gilgamesh, just as a human being burdened with a great task, turns to his god, saying, please let me come home safe again.

With this 'soul' we must be a bit careful, because *nafshu* in Babylonian means soul, but, as in 'I thought in my soul,' it just stands for myself. You have that in Arabic today, and in the Bible you read *Chashavti benafshi*, I thought in my soul, meaning I thought to myself. We cannot put too much weight on this word, although the use of the word is interesting in itself. Here it is a humble, genuine human prayer not praying for more than surviving a task he knows he has to perform. It also has the other aspect, that it is important for him to *know* the danger. Sometimes heroes are very inflated, thinking they can do everything. We will see that Gilgamesh, as a human being, does not quite escape this danger of inflation either, but not at this moment. Do you think it is justified to call this prayer a *rite d'entrée*? It is not exactly a ritual, but as a preparation.

REMARK: It is committing himself, and strengthening.

Yes, and I would also say, with the elders he had to realize the worldly side. Here he has to realize his inner destiny. If he did not, and would not have a human attitude about it, he would be a kind of Icarus flying to the sun. It is very important to see here that Shamash, the son of the moon god Sin, is a sun god. The sun is a symbol of energy and of consciousness, since it enlightens the world. That Shamash is behind the whole enterprise of Gilgamesh is expressly confirmed in the third *rite d'entrée*, namely where Gilgamesh goes with Enkidu to his mother Ninsun, who is a goddess. She is a goddess-priestess at the temple of Shamash, so she is devoted to Shamash. Gilgamesh tells her of his plan, the far journey and battle which he does not know, which he is about to undertake, and asks her to pray to Shamash for him. Her prayer is very beautiful and also important, for the reason just given, and therefore I want to read it to you in full. Incidentally, an interesting note on the longevity of rituals is the fact that the altar on the roof where she goes to pray is also to be found in the Bible, where King Josiah destroys such pagan practices (II Kings, 23:12).

3. A Mother's Prayer

Ninsun entered her chamber.
.....
She put on a garment as befitted her body;
She put on an ornament as befitted her breast;
She put on a ... and was covered with her tiara.
..... ground....
..... she went up on the roof.
She went up to ... Shamash and offered incense.
She brought the offering and raised her hands before Shamash:
"Why didst thou give my son Gilgamesh such a restless heart and
endow him with it?
And now thou hast touched him, and he goes
On a far journey, to the place of Humbaba,
To face a battle which he does not know,
To travel a road which he does not know.
Until the day that he goes and returns,
Until he reaches the cedar forest,
Until he kills fierce Humbaba
And destroys from the land all the evil which thou abhorrest,
The day that thou....
.... may Aya, thy bride, remind thee of it.
Intrust him to the watchmen of the night."

(Tabl. III, col. ii, lines 1-21, Heidel p. 41f)

There are a few very important things in this prayer.

REMARK: She's aware of the necessity...

Yes, she's aware of the higher meaning of this journey. But what is expressed in the very first sentence – "Why didst thou...?"

REMARK: She's ambivalent.

Yes, you can say so, she is ambivalent somewhere, but is it really a resentment? I feel it is an expression of suffering. She knows he has to go, but it is very motherly of her to say "why must *I* have such a son who has to do all these things, why just my son?" It is a timeless story. "Now thou hast touched him" is a very beautiful expression. When the god has touched a mortal, he has to go a way he does not know. This immediacy of being touched by fate, by destiny, is very impressive, showing the reality of being caught by something inner and greater, which forms our life. Psychologically we could say he is touched by the Self. And his mother knows it. She does not talk like the elders. Naturally, being a priestess of Shamash, would mean, psychologically, that she herself is devoted to this principle of higher consciousness. That helps her to let him go, although with pain, but not resisting, not having a small attitude, not wanting "my son" to be just a "normal" man, living in a normal prosaic way. It is a remarkable prayer for a mother, and perhaps it needs some divinity to be such a mother – or also a connection with the Self, which has to do with some divinity. She knows her son is touched by something greater, and there is nothing to do. But it is very humanly described: Why such a restless heart? So he has a restless heart, is not someone who can sit still and be content with all that he has – a kingdom, a city, temples, for he has a restless heart. "Thou hast touched him," and he must go on this far journey – to face a battle he does not know, to travel a road he does not know – which is a classical expression for going the inner way which one does not know. One only knows one has to go it. The

Chinese word *Tao* means "the way" as well as "meaning" or "goal." It is an equilibrium of the opposites. We do not know the meaning except by going the way, step by step. We do not know the goal ahead. We only know we want to come closer to the Self, to become more ourselves. But we cannot know what it is unless we go every step, not knowing where it leads us. Naturally, without that attitude, which needs courage as well as humbleness one does not know. And she does not know. And Gilgamesh does not know.

What they both know is only that he has to go – there is no way out. Of course sometimes one thinks there are ways out. It depends on where they lead. And she also prays to Shamash to protect him, and she says, in a nice little aperçu, that his bride should remind him to protect Gilgamesh. What does she really appeal to? To his feminine side, his feeling. There are other such examples. For instance, in the Old Testament, in the episode with Noah – something which is easily overlooked – Yahweh makes a sign in heaven, the rainbow, to remind *Himself* namely, that He should not destroy mankind again. That is often overlooked. He does not put it there to remind Noah – he will not forget anyway – but that *He* should not forget, and not do something like this again. So Ninsun turns to Shamash and says: "May your bride remind you to protect my son, and entrust him to the watchmen of the night," namely to Sin, his father, the god of the moon, who is really the ruler of the night. What is expressed here symbolically? How does she look at the journey of her son? A night journey. A night sea journey, to use the term of Frobenius. It is the inner way of going into the dark, and we will see how true this is, especially in the second part of our epic. The prayer of Ninsun seems to me to be a classical model for the positive attitude of the personal mother toward the destiny of her son. It is almost superhuman, which means, psychologically, that this attitude can only grow in a person who is related to the Self. It is natural that she suffers through that destiny – "Why didst thou give my son such a restless heart?" but she accepts his fate.

What do we call this attitude psychologically? She's not possessive, but, on the contrary, helpful. Ninsun's prayer therefore is also meaningful because it shows, in the myth itself, the discrimination between the personal mother and the archetypal mother. In reality, she prays to Shamash that he may help her son to overcome the mother! What makes it sometimes so difficult for mothers, especially in the case of the so-called mother complex of the son, is that what he really has to suffer is the archetype behind her, so in relating to the son's attitude, whether positive or negative, she needs must discriminate between the archetype of the mother and herself. If she embodies the archetype she will get all the slavish devotion and/or all the hatred in the most extreme cases. She must know how much she participates in the archetype, and how much not – how much she is a human being. Here we have the personal mother of Gilgamesh; and who is the archetypal mother? Ishtar. She is the archetypal great mother. And they are differentiated here, which will become clearer as we go on. To sum up; this prayer, this third *rite d'entrée,* is, as we have said, to help Gilgamesh to overcome the mother, which is its real psychological meaning, and a classical attitude for a mother. Because if in this sense a son does not overcome the mother, he will remain *in* the mother. Maybe all according to the wishes of the mother, but he will then not gain his manhood.

IV

IN THE CEDAR FOREST

1. Ill-omen at the Gate

In the fourth tablet, whose beginning is missing, we find Gilgamesh and Enkidu at the entrance to the cedar forest. There must have been much in between, probably describing their journey to the forest, but unfortunately, it is missing. The text has many gaps. Before they actually enter the cedar forest they must overcome a watchman guarding the gate, placed there by Humbaba. Gilgamesh, spurred on by Enkidu, apparently succeeds in this, but then something happens, the importance of which will be revealed later on. So there is a guarded gate to this realm, similar to the gate to paradise or the gate to the underworld. In the myth "Ishtar's Descent to the Underworld," there are seven gates through which she must pass, and the motif of the gates of death also occurs in some Psalms (9:13, 107:18). There are gates to the realms where the gods reside. And here, before the cedar forest we have a gate also, the guardian of which has apparently been overcome by our hero. After a gap in the text we next read:

> *Enkidu opened his mouth and spoke, saying to Gilgamesh:*
> *"My friend, let us not go down into the forest.*
> *When I opened the gate, my hand became paralyzed."*
>
> (Tabl. IV, col. vi, lines 23-25, Heidel p. 44)

Why should this happen? How does this strike you? How would a primitive person take this? As soon as he touches the gate and wants to make this transition, he is paralyzed. It is a bad omen! One could say that it is the gods' disagreement, at least, if not revenge, for what the heroes are planning to do. We will later see that it is really the first sign of the revenge of the gods – the gods who later will decide on Enkidu's death because of this. And now we have to recall that Enkidu had the greatest misgivings and uneasiness about going along with Gilgamesh, but was pulled along by him. One has the feeling that this incident at the gate is a bad omen, at least for Enkidu. Gilgamesh is able to cure the paralysis of Enkidu's hand. We do not know how, for the text has a gap here. But he cures his hand, and the hand, as we know, is a symbol of activity. He heals Enkidu's activity. He restores him, one can assume, by some magic spell, though this is not mentioned. The reluctance of Enkidu, and this first sign that, so to speak, he will have to pay the bill for this deed, is natural from a human point of view, for this is, we could say, a break-in, a forceful entry into the divine realm. It is a kind of sacrilegious deed, similar to another sacrilegious deed in Greek mythology, which also had its inner necessity, that of Prometheus. That also had the quality of setting out to do something which affected the gods. We will talk more of this later, when we know more about Enkidu, but this first sign gives us a feeling for the atmosphere we are in here. The text goes on:

> At the green mountain they arrived together;
> Stilled into silence were their words, and they themselves stood still.
> They stood still and looked at the forest.
>
> (Tabl. IV, col. vi, lines 40-42, Heidel p. 45)

Here again is the beauty of that archaic poetry, of which only a few lines are preserved, describing the wonders of the cedar forest, gazing at which struck our heroes speechless, and which expressly confirms the connection between the cedar forest, Humbaba, and Ishtar – here called by another form of her name, Irnini. Tablet five begins:

> *They stood still and looked at the forest.*
> *They beheld the height of the cedar.*
> *They beheld the entrance to the forest.*
> *Where Humbaba was wont to walk there was a path;*
> *Straight were the tracks and good was the passage.*
> *They beheld the mountain of the cedar, the dwelling- place of the*
> *   gods, the throne-dais of Irnini.*
> *The cedar bore its wealth on the slope of the mountain*
> *Fair was its shade and full of delight.*
>
> (Tabl. V, col. i, lines 1-8, Heidel p. 45)

2. The Toppled Mountain

But before they meet Humbaba, Gilgamesh has three dreams. The first is not preserved. The second reads as follows:

> *"Within deep mountain gorges we were standing,*
> *A mountain fell.....*
> *In comparison to it we were like a little 'fly of the canebrakes.' "*
>
> (Tabl. V, col. iii, lines 33-35, Heidel p. 46)

Another version of that dream is a most important continuation. It is from a Semitic rescension from Boghazköy. There it goes on:

> *"In my dream, my friend, a mountain toppled;*
> *It struck me, caught my feet.....*

(And now, most importantly, the lysis, which is missing in the other version:)

> *The light became glaringly strong, a unique man appeared.*

His grace was the most beautiful in all the land.
He pulled me out from under the mountain.
He gave me water to drink, and my heart felt at ease.
On the ground he set my feet....."

(col. iii, lines 13-19, Heidel p. 46f)

This is a very good example for the importance of the
lysis. But first, let us look at the structure of the dream. As
Jung has pointed out, the structure of most dreams is like
that of a Greek drama: there is first an exposition, the
introduction, then a complication, which reaches a high
point, the climax, and then comes the lysis, the solution. He
said on several occasions how important it is that the dream
have a lysis. Dreams that seem not to have, or sometimes
really do not have a lysis, have another character: they do
not show any outcome. Often one wakes up before the lysis.
Jung has pointed out that the very waking up from such a
dream may be considered as the lysis, as though the unconscious says: 'Look, such and such is the case! Now wake up!'
If we are able to wake up to what we saw, that could be the
lysis. But the usual classic dream has these four structural
parts, and looking at it from this point of view is very helpful
in reaching the meaning of the dream. It is not always easy
to know where to make the division of these four parts, but
finding this structure is very helpful for understanding the
quality of the dream. Now looking at these two versions, it is
quite obvious that the Hittite version has a lysis which is
missing in the Babylonian one. In the latter, a mountain fell,
in comparison to which, they were like little flies. Enkidu
interprets this dream as follows:

"*The dream is excellent.....*
My friend, the mountain which thou didst see is Humbaba
We shall seize Humbaba, we shall kill him,
And shall throw his body on the plain."

(Tabl. V, col. iii, lines 39-42, Heidel p. 46)

As the story unfolds, this interpretation proves to be correct, so far as it goes, but the Hittite version, which is longer, goes much further, has a different atmosphere, and its lysis adds an additional element to the picture which makes all the difference in the world. For what does it say? He ended up on his feet. He is saved. It is very concrete. The dream says the mountain topples, but Gilgamesh is saved. Without the second part, the dream would doubtless have been a catastrophe, and it would neither explain Enkidu's interpretation that the dream announces the overcoming of Humbaba, nor would it fit the later course of the epic. There is nevertheless *one* catastrophic aspect: only Gilgamesh is saved. And this implies something else. The lysis says something, but indirectly there is another message in it. It does not say that Enkidu is saved.

It is Gilgamesh's dream, and we will see that this is of importance. Let us go a bit into the symbols in this dream. We will have to confine ourselves to a few allusions, for the very first symbol, the mountain, is so complex one could write a whole essay on it. The mountain can have different meanings. What is it here?

REMARK: A higher consciousness.

I would say so if you think of the mountain as the place of the gods, where it would stand for the Self. But the mountain appears in many dreams where it is not necessarily the Self, but more simply, a higher place from which you have a broader view, a higher view. As in the flood story, where the hero comes to rest on a mountain top, we might say in a state of higher consciousness. Think of Mt. Ararat. We will also see that here, though the mountain has a different name, as also the hero. The mountain then is the symbol of consciousness which rises up as the waters of the unconscious subside. But the mountain is also the symbol of an ascent, one could say to a state of higher consciousness. In analysis people not infrequently dream of a difficult climb to reach a place whence they can see more. Either climbing the mountain or descending into the depths, like in Goethe's Faust, where Mephisto says to him, to Faust: "Now go down to the Mothers. I could also say: 'Climb up.' " Reaching the inner depths is climbing up as well as going down. There are some very complex archetypal symbols, like the mountain, and water, and the snake and the tree, which have many facets, and then we must find which of them best fits the context. That is part of the art of dream interpretation. If we apply a different meaning, which as such may belong to the symbol but is not fitting to the context in the particular dream, it would not open it up – at least, not correctly. Similarly with associations, of which there may be a number. We cannot be sure that the first association is fitting. When people begin to know a bit psychologically, they sometimes do not really associate, but attempt to interpret right away, which may prevent the essential meaning of the dream from coming through. A patient frequently may have several associations, and they may form a significant cluster of meanings, but occasionally there is one which really "clicks," to both the dreamer and the analyst, and that is the one which touches the core of the problem.

Symbols are living structures, and have many facets. As we mentioned, the mountain may imply an ascent, and in our case, the endeavor of the heroes to find and overcome Humbaba, may be so construed. Enkidu, as we have seen, equates the mountain with Humbaba, and sees the fallen mountain as signifying that they will kill him. But there is another aspect to the mountain. What does a mountain consist of? It is stone and also earth. The mountain may be considered as a symbol of the mother, for it also has a feminine quality. In poetry and also in dreams, hills and mountains are sometimes compared with the human body, or with the breasts of a woman. It is also the ascent, the ambition, wanting to climb up high. I would think the mountain here symbolizes the concentrated libido on the overcoming of the mother, of the earth-mother. We recall the heroes' awed silence as they gazed at "the mountain of the cedar, the dwelling-place of the gods, the throne-dais of Irnini" – who is Ishtar, the great mother. And it is there that "Humbaba was wont to walk." *This* climb means to overcome the mother. It could be that libido which is concentrated in the mountain as a symbol of earth. And this mountain topples! The mountain traps Gilgamesh, catches his feet. It is impressive that the very mountain he wants to conquer, topples and immobilizes him. That nature element which symbolizes the undertaking, revenges itself, in effect defeating its would-be victor – by an act of nature – which actually happens on occasion, as for instance in mountain climbing. The venture to overcome the mother is not without real danger. Were the dream to end at this point, it would be conveying a message of, or at least a warning of a catastrophe, which we sometimes get in our dreams. But this whole endeavor being embedded in the divine will does not allow us to think that it is just a preparation for a catastrophe.

And here the lysis is so important, for it shows something other. Gilgamesh, the hero, will be saved. There is, nevertheless, one catastrophic or at least sinister aspect: only Gilgamesh is mentioned. No word about Enkidu, who throughout has been like a second half to Gilgamesh. Heretofore it was always 'we.' Though it was not specified, we are tempted to assume that Enkidu was with Gilgamesh but remained buried under the mountain. In such a case, this dream would anticipate Enkidu's death. We heard earlier of the paralyzing of his hand, and now this dream, by implication, assumes his death. As we will see, later Enkidu himself has a very clear death dream.

Now what about this figure who suddenly appears? This most beautiful light figure who rescues him, gives him water to drink, makes his heart feel at ease, and puts his feet on the ground. What could this figure represent?

REMARK: It sounds like Shamash, which would be indicative of the Self.

Yes, I would say it is a Self figure, coming in a light, and giving him, so to speak, the rescuing water of life. One could say it is the Self as enlightenment, as light. One could also say it is a symbol of the new consciousness which Gilgamesh will reach by his heroic deed, which is with him as a potential – or comes to light in the darkness, namely, when he is buried in that toppled mountain. It is certainly a Self figure, which Shamash also is for Gilgamesh. There is something else we could assume here, if you think of the dynamics of the dream. Enkidu is absent, and this light figure comes into appearance. One could assume a connection here, and what kind of a connection would that be?

REMARK: A transformation.

A transformation! We have that not infrequently. Enkidu is a shadow figure, not only as a negative quality, but as the caring instinct. The shadow, as Jung has shown, is not only the inferior, dark or evil side of the personality, but also the depreciated yet positive potentiality of primitivity and instinctivity. Enkidu is buried now, we might assume, and this light figure comes out. We talked about Enkidu's ambivalence, namely his dark character in the dream of Gilgamesh, and then also his being created in the image of Anu, the sky god. He has a Luciferian quality. It is as if his potential light-bringer quality comes out now. The light hidden in the darkness – think of Enkidu's star character in the first dream – has revealed itself. Perhaps one could see in this light-appearance a figure of the Self into which Enkidu has been changed. It is always the case that the shadow has to be realized before one can reach the Self. Knowing the outcome of the Epic, we can also view the dream as an anticipation of something which will happen; that at the end of the matter Gilgamesh will be put on his feet on the ground by a bright light-figure, that is, a greater consciousness, as we shall see.

3. A Frightful Dream

The two heroes continue on their way, and when they stop for the night, they dig a well before Shamash. Then Gilgamesh, after pouring a sacrifice of fine meal, asks the mountain which he has ascended to bring a dream for Enkidu. The mountain responds, and the numinosity of that event can be felt most clearly in what follows:

A cold shower passed by....
It caused him to cower and....
.... and like the grain of the mountains....
Gilgamesh supports his chin on his knees.

(Tabl. V, col. iv, lines 3-6, Heidel p. 47)

So he is hit by a cold shower. He cowers, crouches, falls asleep, but awakens in the middle of the night, arises and says to Enkidu:

"My friend, didst thou not call me? Why did I wake up?
Didst thou not touch me? Why am I frightened?
Did no god pass by?
Why are my members benumbed with fear?"

(lines 10-12, Heidel p. 47)

Here we have a very impressive description of a numinous experience. He thinks a god passed by. You can see how real it is for him, for he thinks Enkidu touched him. Something touched him. He is awakened in a fright and has the feeling that a god passed by. It is an immediate image of the numinous experience. We have a well known parallel in the Bible of this immediacy – but without the fear, probably because of his childish innocence – when the child Samuel is called by name three times (1st Sam. 3) when he lay down to sleep in the temple, and each time goes to old Eli saying: "Here am I." Each time Eli tells him "I called not; lie down again." till it finally dawns on him that it is God calling him, and he instructs Samuel to answer the next time, if he is called, with the words: "Speak, Lord, for Thy servant heareth." The Bible description of this immediacy is so clearly self-evident: "...and Samuel was laid down to sleep ... the Lord called Samuel; and he said: 'Here am I.' And he ran unto Eli, and said: 'Here am I; for thou didst call me.' " Something like this happens to Gilgamesh. And now he tells Enkidu the dream:

> "My friend, I saw a third dream;
> And the dream which I saw was altogether frightful.
> The heavens roared, the earth resounded;
> Daylight failed, darkness came;
> Lightning flashed, fire blazed;
> The clouds thickened, raining death.
> The brightness vanished, the fire went out;
> And that which fell down, turned to ashes."

(lines 13-20, Heidel p. 47f)

Enkidu interprets the dream to Gilgamesh, but unfortunately, his words are not preserved. Now let us go into this dream. What kind of a dream is it?

REMARK: A disastrous dream.

A disaster! This is a disastrous dream. Again it shows a catastrophe, but this time – what is the difference? There is a very striking difference.

REMARK: It ends in ashes rather than in recovery.

Yes, it has a negative lysis, but in the whole character of the dream there is another feature which I would like to point out. It is on a larger, cosmic scale. As you realize, no human being is to be found in the whole dream. In the other dreams we have Enkidu, and Gilgamesh, and a light figure, but here there is no being at all, neither human nor divine. What is the symbolism, what is the picture of this catastrophe: "The heavens roared, the earth resounded, daylight failed, darkness came, lightning flashed, fire blazed, the clouds thickened, raining death, the brightness vanished, the fire went out, and that which fell down, turned to ashes."

REMARK: The elements of nature.

Yes, and we have some allusions.

REMARK: It is apocalyptic.

It is apocalyptic, but as a picture it could be a tremendous earthquake or a volcanic eruption. The image could be that of a volcanic eruption with fire, raining ashes. But you are absolutely right. It is an apocalyptic happening, a Gotterdämmerung we could say, a twilight of the gods. If we keep this association of a twilight of the gods, what does it mean psychologically?

REMARK: It could mean a complete upheaval of the old, or the overthrow of the old.

Yes, yes, I would say so too. We can expect a deeper meaning which is revealed here to Gilgamesh, that the realm of the old gods passes away. Either something new comes up or not; that we do not know. Very often it is so when a new era comes up and an old one finishes.

In the second dream – the first one is lost to us – Enkidu saw in the toppling mountain the downfall of Humbaba: "We shall seize Humbaba, we shall kill him." Now let's think again of Humbaba. He has some connection with what is pictured here. If we think of Humbaba's fire-breath, which causes death, which Enkidu described at the beginning, and his being an earth-spirit, these qualities could lead us on the path of seeing Humbaba as a personification of that older era which disappears, or is meant to disappear, by the heroic deed. He is, as you remember, the guardian of Ishtar's sacred place, so he could well be that old chthonic masculine spirit belonging to the Great Mother, who goes under in this twilight of the gods. If we are on the right track it is not difficult to think of who would be the upcoming new god. We can guess from what we heard previously and which will be fully confirmed in the following, that it must be *Shamash.* It was Shamash who sent Gilgamesh on the way to kill Humbaba. He had 'touched' Gilgamesh, as his mother Ninsun said, so that he set out "to face a battle which he did not know, and to travel a road which he did not know." Here the very essence of the hero appears in its full meaning: the symbol of man awakening to new consciousness, set on his way by the sun god, driven by the sun god, who is the god of consciousness. Shamash is the spiritual impetus which draws man out of the lethargy of the eternally circling cycle of nature, which is symbolized by the mother goddess.

It was very interesting to me to see how close one commentator came to this understanding, although not writing from a psychological point of view. The Dutch scholar Böhl, in his important book on the Gilgamesh Epic, assumes that the whole epic is an expression of a theological conflict between Uruk, where the goddess Ishtar rules, and Larsa, the center of the worship of the sun god. The epic, from a theological, political viewpoint, expresses the fight between Shamash as an ethical moral god, the god of justice, and the unaccountable, earth goddess Ishtar with her vegetation rites. He raises the question as to why it should be just Gilgamesh, the king of Uruk, which is Ishtar's capitol, who fights the Great Mother. Böhl really gets himself into a tight spot there, and his solution is that it makes the outcome more effective if it is the king of the center of Ishtar worship himself who fights Ishtar. I was interested to read this, for what Böhl says is really so. He sees the thing correctly, in that this is really a competition between the two gods, but he misses the psychologically important point that it is Gilgamesh the *hero* who must overcome Ishtar; not just the most important citizen of Uruk, but the carrier of a new consciousness, the new consciousness of Shamash, that must overcome her.

REMARK: Would not the fact that the matriarchal society is passing also point to his commentary?

Yes, absolutely, but you know, I find it a bit questionable to use the terms matriarchal and patriarchal. I do not like to use these terms, for it is still quite controversial as to what they really mean. I prefer to say the era of the mother goddess, which is not merely or only matriarchal. It is not that simple.

REMARK: Oh, well, instead of saying matriarchal, you can put it another way: it's only when the father takes over that the spiritual comes in.

Yes, yes. In that I would absolutely agree with you, and I think that *that* is what the Gilgamesh Epic really represents. It is a myth giving an invaluable insight into a transition in a religious development; I would say a transition from polytheism into, or toward, monotheism. We will see that when we draw some parallels with the Old Testament. We will see that the Biblical God has some parallels with Shamash, the light bringer, the masculine god. In the comparison of the flood stories of the Epic and the Bible, it will be visible that in the Biblical God there are still elements of the other former gods, but – and that is the great thing – united in one divine personality. It shows a higher consciousness than when the totality of the divine qualities is just met in particles, as it is in polytheism. We have the same thing in an unconscious personality when one can be this one, one day, and on another day, another one. What we try to do in the inner process of development is to unite them into one consciousness. Therefore in active imagination, for instance, that technique of consciously participating in phantasy expressions of the unconscious, certain aspects of ourselves appear as figures, and if we are able to realize them as belonging to ourselves, we pay by the suffering of conflict. We must stand it that we are this, and/but also that, but that is what creates higher consciousness. If you think of very unconscious people, they can be very happy, just like animals, because one day the sun shines, and the next day it rains, and there is no continuation necessarily of an ego carrying all these states. Today I am this one and I am whole, tomorrow I am the other one and I am whole. Naturally that saves one from conflict, but it does not lead to higher consciousness – and usually life does not allow us to play that game for too long.

Here in this hero's dream, we already see the tremendous revolution from the mother world to the father world, at work. The mother world goes under. A thousand years later it is the sun hero Marduk who kills the primeval mother Tiamat, and creates heaven and earth out of the two halves of her body as a new creation. Well, I do not want to say exactly a thousand years later, but the name Marduk does not appear in the Gilgamesh Epic, which is one of the signs that the Epic is older than the Marduk legend. Marduk is the young sun god in Assyrian times, and we do not know how old the Tiamat myth is. It also has Sumerian sources, but in the form with Marduk as its hero, it is younger than the Gilgamesh Epic. From Marduk there is a clear line which leads to the Bible father god, Yahweh, a line which can be traced in the Bible itself. In Job 26:12 we read that Yahweh killed the sea dragon Rahab (which is a synonym for Tiamat) by his *binah*, by his understanding, and this whole image is a parallel to that of Marduk slaying Tiamat with his arrow, with a piercing, discriminating weapon. This image in Job, and Job is a late book in the Old Testament, is a mirroring of the sun hero overcoming the maternal chaos. There is a tendency to not sufficiently acknowledge the mythological imagery in the Bible. One German New Testament scholar has even written about de-mythologizing the Bible. It is a pity to look at it this way, because there is myth also in the Bible, only of another kind. It is not a matter of not recognizing the mythological character, but of realizing the *meaning* of the new myth. A rationalistic trend is visible here, which is also shared by other theologians.

4. Felling the Cedar, and the Fight with Humbaba

What follows is the fight of the heroes with Humbaba, the description of which is lacking in the Nineveh text. But the Hittite version again contains a valuable passage which fills in the gap, from which we learn that things did not go so smoothly:

> *Gilgamesh took the axe in his hand*
> *And cut down the cedar.*
> *But when Huwawa heard the noise,*
> *He became enraged and said: "Who has come*
> *And disturbed the trees that have grown up on my mountains,*
> *And has cut down the cedar?"*

(And now, in the decisive moment when the two heroes are in a very bad spot, Shamash intervenes in an encouraging way:)

> *Then the heavenly Shamash spoke to them*
> *From heaven: "Approach,*
> *Be not afraid...."*

> (Tabl. V, col. iv, lines 7-15, Heidel p. 48)

I would like to mention that this formula, "Be not afraid," in Hebrew *al tira*, occurs frequently in the Bible when an angel or God Himself appears, which shows the numinosity evoked by divinity. People were afraid they would die when and because an angel appeared to them. So when Manoah, Samson's father, realized that it was an angel of the Lord who had appeared to them (Judges 13:20ff.), for he as-

cended heavenward in the flame of the sacrifice, he said to
his wife: "We shall surely die, because we have seen God."
Also at the revelation at Mt. Sinai, enveloped in lightning
and thunder and the sound of the shofar (horn), the people
said to Moses (Ex. 20:16): "Speak thou with us, and we will
hear; but let not God speak with us, lest we die." They feared
to die in meeting the numinous, and the mountain was
numinous too.

Now in the Hittite version as well, there is, unfortunately,
a large gap. The heroes have apparently gotten into great
difficulty, for we find Gilgamesh, after the gap, praying, in
tears, to Shamash:

> *His tears gushed forth in streams.*
> *And Gilgamesh said to the heavenly Shamash:*
> .... [badly damaged]
> .... [" "]
> *I have followed the heavenly Shamash,*
> *And have pursued the road decreed for me."*
>
> (lines 6-11, Heidel p. 48)

In other words, 'and now you let me down.' For it is a
critical phase in the fight. But now Shamash intervenes
helpfully. He sends eight winds which attack Humbaba from
all sides, so that he is no longer able to move, and has to
submit. This detail significantly connects this event with the
other great Babylonian myth, the creation myth, *Enuma elish*, where Marduk overcomes the primeval mother goddess.
I bring this amplification, because the structure of the happening is further evidence, if we did not already know it
from other connections, that Humbaba really stands for the
mother world. In the *Enuma elish*, in the fourth tablet, Marduk also sends out all the winds – there they are seven –
against Tiamat. The wind, as a weapon, fights the mother
monster. What kind of symbol is the wind? Wind is spirit, as
we have it in language. In Hebrew, *ruach* means spirit and

also wind, as does the Arabic *ruh,* which is the same word, and the Greek *pneuma.* In the Bible it is sometimes difficult to know whether to translate the word as wind, or spirit. In our text, these winds are the symbol of a new divine spirit which helps the hero to fight the old spirit. Another analogy or amplification which comes close here, is the Mercurial spirit in the bottle, in the story which Jung has so masterfully interpreted in his essay "The Spirit Mercurius." In that story, the Grimm's fairy tale "The Spirit in the Bottle," the bad spirit who is tricked back in the bottle, also tries to get out of it by promising a rich reward to the boy who had found him. In the same way, Humbaba tries to save his own life by offering his services to Gilgamesh, if he'll let him live. He says:

> *"Let me go, Gilgamesh; thou shalt be my master,*
> *And I will be thy servant. And the trees*
> *That I have grown on my mountains,*
> *......*
> *I will cut down and build thee houses."*
>
> (Tabl. V, col. iv, lines 22-26, Heidel p. 49)

With what does he lure him? With material values. 'I'll make you rich!' Which is naturally also an expression of the material values of the earth spirit. But it is *Enkidu* who warns Gilgamesh:

> *"Do not hearken to the word which Huwawa has spoken:*
> *Huwawa must not remain alive!"*
>
> (lines 28/29-30, Heidel p. 49)

This shows very beautifully how again and again the hero is subjected to the temptation to fall for material values. It is very understandable that sometimes, when tempted, regressive desires come up. 'Why should I not have it this way,' one could think. 'It is nicer.' Here Huwawa is a chthonic spirit who says: 'Look, let me go and I will be like your *familiaris* who can help you get whatever you want. These very trees which you want to extirpate, I will build you houses from them, something very useful and nice to have.' How do you understand that it is just Enkidu who warns him not to do it? One could think it would be just the other way around. Once this spirit of Enkidu, this instinct, has grasped the task, the instinct, which is conservative, cannot so easily be swayed away from it again. Having once caught on, it is now the perseverance in the task. Subjectively spoken, once it has gone so deep as to reach the Enkidu layer, it cannot any more be lightly deterred. As long as something is just an ideal in our heads, it can stumble over a nothing, and be off it again. But once it goes very deep, and the instinct is convinced and drawn in, then it will not let you go so quickly, and that is also a protection against backsliding.

The text breaks off here, but from the damaged Assyrian version, as Heidel writes, "we can conclude that Gilgamesh and Enkidu cut off the head of Humbaba and that the expedition had a successful issue. The two friends then returned to Uruk." (p. 49)

V

GILGAMESH AND ISHTAR

1. Ishtar's Proposal

The following tablet, the sixth, again represents a climax in the abundant episodes of the myth. Namely, Ishtar, the mighty goddess, up to now the invisible center of the whole flow of events, finally appears personally. It always reminds me of a well structured drama; the power, the grey eminence, does not appear in the first act, but in the middle. Ishtar is the whole background of all the proceedings, and now comes the climax: she appears. And she woos Gilgamesh. Gilgamesh has come back from his successful heroic enterprise, has washed himself and put on clean garments, and the text goes on:

> *When Gilgamesh put on his tiara,*
> *Great Ishtar lifted up her eyes to the beauty of Gilgamesh.*
> *"Come, Gilgamesh, be thou my consort.*
> [variants: bridegroom; lover]
> *Grant me thy fruit as a gift.*
> *Be thou my husband and I will be thy wife!*
> *I will cause to be harnessed for thee a chariot of lapis lazuli and gold,*
> *Whose wheels are gold and whose horns are....*
> *Storm-demons for great mules thou shalt hitch to it.*
> *Amid the fragrance of cedar thou shalt enter our house.*
> *And when thou enterest our house,*
> *Threshold and dais shall kiss thy feet.*

Before thee shall bow down kings, rulers, and princes.
The yield of mountain and plain they shall bring thee in tribute.
Thy goats shall bear triplets, thy sheep twins.
Thy donkey shall go its way with the load of a mule.
Thy chariot horses shall be famous for their running.
Thine ox in the yoke shall have no rival."

(Tabl. VI, lines 5-21, Heidel p. 49f)

What is the atmosphere of this proposal? It has a certain luscious grandeur. What does she promise? Power and wealth. The richest fantasies imaginable. She promises him, in accordance with her essential nature, all the treasures of the earth. It is extraordinarily interesting that Ishtar should come in – and even with her wooing – just at this moment. Gilgamesh has just, so to speak, killed her! Symbolically. He has fulfilled his first heroic deed. He has felled the cedar, and killed Humbaba. So we can say that, symbolically, he has overcome the mother. And now she comes up as great and as rich and as powerful and as seducing as ever. What has happened here? The key lies in a factor which leads beyond her mother quality. How does she appear here? What does she want from Gilgamesh? She does not say 'Oh, come now, come back. I'm your mother and you are my loving son.' She does not want him just to come back and say 'Sorry.' She comes back with all the luring of a woman. She says come, be my husband, and you will have a most wonderful life. So something happened in Ishtar; another aspect has come to the foreground. It is not quite new, for we have seen that the kings were the husbands of the goddess, but symbolically. You recall that when Enkidu and Gilgamesh met, Gilgamesh wanted to enter the family house to unite with the goddess Ishhara (represented by a hierodule), an aspect of Ishtar. But here there is a directness which brings out more clearly another quality of Ishtar, because also Ishhara was the mother. Here it is expressly the lover aspect. One could say it is another anima aspect coming into view in the goddess. As Jung has shown, the first anima experience of the son is the mother, and the anima as such comes later in his development. Here we have in Ishtar another quality which we can relate to the psychological fact that the mother, the earliest form of the anima, is first replaced by a mother-like woman. A kind of mother-lover. Quite often in the case of men with strong mother-complexes, love will first fall on a woman who is either much older, or who has outspoken motherly qualities. Naturally the development of the relationship will depend on the development of other qualities in the woman. Failing that, the man will stay stuck in the mother even though he is married and not living with the mother.

In our text it is the same Ishtar, but in another aspect of the archaic richness of this divine figure. Ishtar represents the fullness of all feminine aspects in the germ, as it were, not yet unfolded, as we will see later on, when we will meet other features. She is really the whole feminine potential. Although there are certain goddesses who are already differentiated aspects of her, she still contains all of them in herself as the most powerful goddess in the Babylonian pantheon. Gilgamesh's answer to her is of epoch-making importance, looked at from the point of view of the development of human consciousness. He declines Ishtar's offer with unheard of bitterness and cynicism.

2. Gilgamesh's Rebuff

Gilgamesh's answer to Ishtar's proposal is immediate and unsparing. He rhetorically asks the great Ishtar what he must give her if he takes her in marriage, and duly notes that they include oil and clothes for her body, and bread and victuals; food which is fit for divinity as well as drink appropriate for royalty. Following a break in the text of a few lines, he asks what would be *his* advantage from a marriage with her, and then proceeds to describe her in no uncertain terms:

"Thou art but a ... which does not ... in the cold;
A back door which does not keep out blast or windstorm;
A palace which crushes the heroes within it;
An elephant that shakes off his carpet;
Pitch which dirties him who carries it;
A waterskin which wets him who carries it:
.....
.....
A shoe which pinches the foot of its wearer;"

(Tabl. VI, lines 33-41, Heidel p. 50)

Following this harsh yet poetically picturesque flow of accusations and denunciatory comparisons, he moves to her personal feelings – or lack of them.

"What lover of thine is there whom thou dost love forever?
What shepherd of thine is there who can please thee for all time?
Come, and I will unfold thee the tale of thy lovers.
For Tammuz, thy youthful husband,
Thou hast decreed wailing year after year."

(Tabl. VI, lines 42-7, Heidel p. 50f)

This is because Tammuz has been killed. The remark "you have decreed wailing" for him, has to do with the ancient ritual in which women mourn his death, and in the spring rejoice over his resurrection. (Mention of this rite occurs in the Bible, in Ezekiel 8:14, where the prophet in a vision is brought from Babylon to the temple in Jerusalem, "and, behold, there sat the women weeping for Tammuz." During their exile in Babylon, the Jews named the fourth month in their calendar, Tammuz, which falls mostly during July.) Every year women wail for him when he is killed by the destructive heat which Ishtar is in the summer. In the spring Ishtar is the veiled bride. She has these two aspects. Having referred to her yearly slaying of her youthful husband, Gilgamesh then turns to the animals she loved.

"The variegated roller thou didst love.
Yet thou didst smite him and break his wing.
Now he stands in the groves, crying 'Kappi!'
Thou didst love the lion, perfect in strength.
But thou didst dig for him seven and yet seven pits.
Thou didst love the horse, magnificent in battle.
Yet thou hast decreed for him the whip, the spur, and the lash.
To run seven double-hours thou hast decreed for him.
Thou hast decreed for him to trouble the water before drinking it.
For his mother Silili thou hast decreed lamentation."

(Tabl. VI, lines 48-57, Heidel p.51)

An especially interesting picture of Ishtar's nature is in connection with the bird crying "Kappi, Kappi," my wing, my wing! This was Ishtar's lover whose wings she had broken. Psychologically spoken, she had broken the spiritual wings of her son-lover. I am reminded of a dream of a woman who, due to difficult circumstances, had to give up her studies. After a few years she dreamed that she was back at the university, and an animus figure appeared – a young man who had been a fellow student of hers. He is now walking with her and his arms are in splints. They had been broken and are now in the process of healing. That dream was a sign for her to resume her studies, which she later did. Birds move in the air, a spiritual medium, and so are a symbol of spiritual thoughts, or intuitions, (flights of fancy), and a broken wing, as you can see from the dream, means an inability to fly in the realm of the spirit. Now criticism had broken his wing, and this too, happens fairly often – that the spiritual impulse and desire are broken by the common sense and all-too-matter-of-fact attitude of the mother. Jung once said that women are not sufficiently aware of the fact that by their common sense and down-to-earthness, so highly praised in other connections, they can kill the fantasy of man, or his spiritual impulses – by putting on them the damp cloth of their insufficiently understanding "practicality." Women should know their effect on men, just as men, in another way, should be conscious of their effect on women. It is most important that we learn to be aware of how we affect others, and not only how others affect us.

Gilgamesh is not yet finished with his catalogue of Ishtar's reprehensible behavior. He continues his enumeration, turning now to her human lovers.

> *"Thou didst love the shepherd of the herd,*
> *Who without ceasing heaped up breadcakes for thee.*
> *And daily slaughtered kids for thee.*
> *Yet thou didst smite him and turn him into a wolf.*
> *His own herd boys now chase him away,*
> *And his dogs bite his shanks.*
> *Thou didst love Ishullanu, thy father's palm-gardener,*
> *Who without ceasing brought thee baskets filled with dates*
> *And daily provided thy table with plenty.*
> *Thou didst cast thine eyes on him and didst go to him, saying:*
> *'My dear Ishullanu, come, let us enjoy thy vigor.*
> *Put forth thy hand and touch our waist.'*
> *Ishullanu said to thee:*
> *'What dost thou ask of me?*
> *Does my mother not bake? Have I not eaten,*
> *That I should eat bread of stinking and rotten things?*
> *Do bulrushes afford sufficient protection against the cold?'*
> *When thou didst hear this, his speech,*
> *Thou didst smite him and transform him into a mole.*
> *Thou didst cause him to dwell in the middle of ...*
> *He does not ascend the ..., he does not go down....*
> *And if thou wilt love me, thou wilt treat me like unto them."*
>
> (Tabl. VI, lines 58-79, Heidel p. 51f)

In this description, as you see, Ishtar appears in her full light.

What does he tell her she did with her lovers? What did she do? She destroyed them. Either she killed them, or she changed them into animals, and humiliated them in that way. She appears here as the devouring destroying mother-lover. Gilgamesh really gives her a full account of all her evil deeds with her lovers. What does it mean if they are changed into animals? One has been changed into a wolf, and another into a mole, digging under the earth and not seeing the light of the day. Think of the animal nature of Enkidu, which he had to overcome. Here they are changed into a pre-human fate. It is a regression to a sub-human level, so to speak. Her victims are banished into a mere animal existence. They fall back, one could say, to the circle or cycle of nature, into the realm of the animal existence in the mother, just instinctive beings. Animals can often appear as positive symbols, but to change into an animal is a regression to a pre-human existence. You can see that all these animals are not living a free life. The horse must drink the water he has first muddied, the bird has a broken wing. The symbolism is negative. Even as animals they are afflicted with a humiliation or restriction of a free natural existence.

Gressmann, in his commentary to the epic, in referring to this transformation motif, mentions (p.125, n.4) an interesting example given by St. Augustine, who tells of women innkeepers in Italy who served cheese to their guests, which, by a magic spell turned them into mares. This is very interesting, for here, too, we have the symbolism of the horse. But the mare, as the female animal, has a strong connection with the negative aspect of the goddess as the mother goddess. Symbolically they have been changed into the instinctive power of themselves, they become a piece of themselves. St. Augustine describes how the innkeepers used the mares they had turned their guests into, to work for them. That is what a mother complex can do, as in *Der Tote Tag*, by Barlach, where the son becomes a function of the mother. She says to him: "I cannot live without you, and if you want to go away, I will kill you!" which she did by killing the horse given to him by his father, which should carry him out into the world. That is the Dead Day – the morning in which this heinous deed is committed, at the instigation of that Steissbarth, *familiaris animus,* which turned the son insane. This is an instance of the typical happening when the mother goddess has the power over these son-lovers, to change them into servants for herself.

More than we dream of, this cruel archetypal pattern is hidden behind more inconspicuous relationships between mothers and sons. A current example is that of an old widowed ("witch") mother who kept her son, her "great treasure" as she called him, as her bachelor servant, until he was in his late sixties, when she finally died. After which, as he confided, he "felt like an orphan"! In addition to her positive maternal qualities, being merciful, protecting in childbirth, etc., Ishtar also has this aspect of devouring her children – her sons. This example from St. Augustine is especially illuminating on account of the fact that Ishtar herself is also an inn-keeper, as we shall see. We will find her in the form of Siduri, the "bar-maid," as Heidel translates it, whom Gilgamesh meets later in his travels.

The transformation of people into animals is a frequent fairy tale and mythical motif, and the nearest to hand here is the well-known story of Circe, who turned Odysseus' sailors into swine – who always have their heads close to the ground, their noses in the dirt. And just this example of Odysseus gives us an extraordinarily interesting insight into the development of myths as documents of the development of human consciousness. The Odyssey is a younger myth. In its written form it is dated at about 1,000 B.C.E., whilst the Gilgamesh Epic's Sumerian roots go back to about 4,000 B.C.E. One could say that the encounter with the woman, or the anima, in psychological terms, has an altogether different character. That makes it so fascinating also, quite apart from the beauty of the myths, to compare them, because we can realize different sets of the same archetypal pattern. Circe is also a powerfully seductive female figure and she changes the man who cannot stand up to her, into a swine. But obviously Odysseus is in a different position than Gilgamesh. He can, as it were, accept Circe's wooing, under certain cautious conditions. He does not just give her a horrible rebuff as Gilgamesh did, who, apart from his reproach that Ishtar changes her lovers into animals, says, "What do I have to give you if I marry you? You are unreliable." To return to the text:

> *"What will be my advantage if I take thee in marriage?*
> *Thou art but a ... which does not ... in the cold;*
> *A back door which does not keep out blast or windstorm;*
> *A palace which crushes the heroes within it;*
> *An elephant that shakes off his carpet;*
> *Pitch which dirties him who carries it;" etc.*
>
> (Tabl. VI, lines 32-37, Heidel p. 50)

He makes all these horrible accusations, and he just leaves her there. The hero Odysseus, in a different position, as was said, accepts Circe's invitation; but he has the divine help of Hermes, who gave him the miraculous herb Moly to foil her drugs, and who instructed him to charge her with his sword when she tried to bewitch him. What would it mean that he has his sword with him? The sword is symbol of discrimination. So he has a certain awareness of the situation. The sword is naturally also a weapon with which to defend himself, which would mean that a certain insight of the hero is necessary in order to be able to stand up against this sucking in of the mother, also against her seductive powers. Having his sword with him symbolizes the man's strength of discrimination and insight, his capability of being conscious of what's going on. Then he can go.

REMARK: Would you call it a symbol of will-power and intention?

Well, I would not really, even though it has something to do with it, for you can have the will to overcome something, yet not the insight necessary. So we can see the difference in the attitudes of the heroes of two different myths of different times, in the same situation, so to speak. One could say that what would be certain death for Gilgamesh, namely to accept Ishtar's invitation, as we have seen from all the examples he mentioned, is nevertheless possible for Odysseus. Since the sword is a Logos symbol in this connection, it is obvious that it is a higher level of consciousness which enables Odysseus to tolerate or admit an encounter which Gilgamesh was not up to. Gilgamesh, on the other hand, was the first in a long line of heretofore killed son-lovers who was able to stand up to the danger to the extent of being able to spurn and reject it, if not to run away. This shows how careful one must be in similar situations, for example, with analysands. For the one it may be a life necessity to escape the situation, and for the other it may be a life necessity to meet the danger. It depends on the level of consciousness. We can never make rules. Naturally, for a modern man, one might say, well, he cannot just run away. That does not solve the anima problem. But if he is in a Gilgamesh state, he has to.

Once in a children's dream seminar of Jung's, we dealt with a dream of a young boy which anticipated a later development during puberty, in which he saw an anima figure dead in the water, and he had a feeling of separation pain, but he went away. Jung said then that in certain situations, when the anima figure or the mother is too powerful, the only thing a man can do is to avoid it at the time, and wait until he is up to it. Otherwise he is just fooling himself. There are men who think they made it, and are not aware how much, despite their achievements, they are caught in the mother. We will see later in the epic how Gilgamesh and Enkidu fulfill a ritual which is a symbol of *really* breaking free of the mother. In these examples we can glimpse the psychological importance of the comparative method of myth interpretation. But we must know that all these myths stand for certain stages of development, for in comparing them with dream material, we must know what we are comparing. There is always a correspondence at certain levels of consciousness, in which a particular attitude is given, and not in other cases. Jung once said to me that if someone were listening in to a row of analytical sessions, he would be utterly bewildered by hearing the analyst say to one person the absolute opposite of what he had said to another in the previous hour. This is because life is manifold, and it depends on what, among the many possible truths referring to human life, is *the* truth at this moment for this person. In dream interpretation, we must be very careful not to apply some a-priori idea to a dream, for the dream might just have an altogether surprising view of a certain situation, not the expected one we are in danger of mistakenly making, identifying what's really at stake in the situation. We can have perfectly wonderful convictions about a psychological situation, which, however, do not fit, because we can miss the point. Thank goodness, the dreams usually correct it. Learning to discriminate in dealing with myths, can help us in learning to discriminate with dreams.

REMARK: Would that imply that individuation could not be accomplished in that collective type at that time?

3. On Individuation Goals

You are right in what you mean, but I would formulate it a little differently. You see, it is always individuation, but the goal is different at certain states. Individuation for Gilgamesh is, in the first place, to free himself from the mother. We might ask: when does individuation begin? I think it begins at birth. It is a natural process of growth. But the goal of individuation in the first half of life is very different from the goal in the second half of life. There is a frequent misunderstanding that Jungian psychology is especially for the second half of life, and that then is when individuation begins. Individuation is the innate drive for completeness. For a young person, finding roots in life belongs to individuation. Otherwise, what we think is individuation in the second half of life, is twisted, because something has not been fulfilled, has not been grounded. We must discriminate what belongs to individuation in certain phases of life, and that we can learn only from dreams. Naturally, there are young people who have dreams indicating that they must do something that is not the so-called normal way. But then that is their individuation way. And then we see many dreams of young people who are very fascinated by the unconscious, yet what they have to do first is something else – and then *that* is their individuation. We cannot skip classes in the unconscious. We have to go through the whole process.

Another way of putting it is that the individuation task is proposed by the unconscious. There are certain general typical situations which we can say are more or less the same for everybody. But we are not of the same inner composition. Even not the same age; we speak of people who are younger or older than they are in some way. This is also true about our contemporaries. We are not all living in the same time. We sometimes meet people where one has the feeling that they would have been much happier, with their inner make up, living in the age of Romanticism, or even in antiquity. Individuation is something highly individual, as the word indicates. This is why we must rely on the unconscious, and must be as careful as possible not to interpret unconscious material according to ideas we fancy about the individuation process. They are a help. We must have some guiding conceptions, which we have. Jung himself was a most wonderful example for never being excessively systematical or making rigid rules, although he created a view of certain connections which are typical – which are arche*typal* as such. In the single case he was always open to exceptions or very individual situations where one could miss the point if one would say "Now this *should* come." Nothing "should" come. It comes as it is, and then we can see what we have to do with it. But to come back to our myth: it is very important to have such patterns. There is not only a Gilgamesh, and we never could say that the hero *should* reject his mother. Nor is there always an Odysseus. There are also men who cannot afford it because they would not be up to it at this moment. As you know, in the unconscious, in our inner processes, we are led in a roundabout way, not in a straight line as we sometimes would like or expect. So Gilgamesh, I feel, had to do what he did, which is no pattern or specific example as such for man's individuation process.

But there is a phase where this is the one necessity, as with Gilgamesh, where the mother was so threatening and negative. With him it is a matter, so to speak, of the *first* attempt to get out of the maternal cycle of nature, into a new spiritual development. There is an early essay by Albright, the outstanding American scholar of the orient, the author of *From the Stone Age to Christianity*, in which he says that Gilgamesh was himself a vegetation god in line with Tammuz and others. He shows similarities, and as we have seen here, Gilgamesh looks at Tammuz as a predecessor among Ishtar's lovers. So then he would be another Tammuz, but one who breaks the pattern. This is an epochal encounter. He breaks the pattern of being swallowed by the mother, and this is his greatness, this is his individuation task. He can not afford anything else. It is usually so: that you have to do the utmost that you can. But you cannot do the impossible. If our consciousness is in a certain state, you can only do that much. The challenge is anyhow usually somewhat beyond us. But if it is too far beyond us, we just cannot do it at that moment. Something more has to happen before we can do more. It may seem like a defeat, but to accept a defeat, if it is necessary, can be more heroic than being light-heartedly caught in something one is not up to. Psychologically spoken, I see Gilgamesh's accomplishment as *the* heroic achievement at this time. It was really breaking the pattern, which opened a new vista, a new development out of the motherly circle of nature into a new spiritual development. Naturally, if we allow ourselves to utter such an intuition, it must be proven in the continuation of the myth, which I think it is.

4. Mother-World, Mother-Complex

It is a decisive turning point, one could say a cultural turning point, for he is a culture hero, and therefore back-sliding into the mother-world, once it is overcome, would be *the* great danger for him. For modern consciousness such behavior towards the mother anima would not be adequate in general, except in a psychic situation which corresponds to the level of this given setting. For instance, the more or less modern situation, especially in America, of juvenile delinquency, or the great emphatic independence of youth, of which juvenile delinquency is one branch; seeing it as belonging to the attempt to break away from the pattern of having to be a good boy – and then going overboard to being a bad boy. But if you see it in this connection, if you see the pathetic, almost tragic fight to break the pattern of dependence, you get another view of it. Naturally, changing this pattern depends a good deal on the insight of the parents. On the other hand, you could also read, as was more than once written, that the lack of a father is a big factor in the problem of juvenile delinquency. But it boils down to the same problem. If the father does not fill his fatherly role, he has missed helping his son to achieve his masculinity. It needs insight on the sides of both women and men, about their role, all over the world. Remember the attitude of Ninsun toward Gilgamesh, in letting him go. She lets him "get onto his horse" and get into the world. This is also a precondition to enable him to stand up to Ishtar. Being free of his personal mother does not automatically make a man free of the mother archetype. This discrimination between the personal mother and the archetypal mother in this old epic is fantastic. Some men coming to analysis say: "But I do not live with my mother, and we have a very nice relationship," or "I do not like her. Therefore I left home, and I'm free." And the dreams are full of negative mother symbols. That problem is something which cannot be dealt with by just a geographical separation. It goes with one. The mother complex shows itself not only in dependence on the personal mother or a mother figure. Life, or an analyst, becomes the mother. It is an attitude of wanting always to be served, of not wanting to take any trouble. That, in the last extent, is a clear sign of a mother-complex attitude. It goes way beyond the personal. Even the personal mother, behaving in a positive or negative form of the mother archetype, is, unless she is aware of the role she is playing, a victim of the archetype. Here is an advantage of Jung's broader view of the psyche. It gets one out of the mill of endlessly reproaching the personal parents, as some people unfortunately suffer from all their lives, which is just too sad and unfruitful. The archetypes are really the inner powers to which we must find an apt relationship. All people, mothers as well as sons, are caught in the same archetypes, and have at their own end to struggle with them. I think it has been worthwhile to dwell on this matter in order to show that the myth cannot be explained without the point of view of the development of consciousness. That is the point of reference. Just as a dream can not really be fully explained without the point of reference of the conscious situation of the dreamer. And when we do not know it, as for example with a mythical hero, we can, from the dream, surmise what the state of consciousness must be for such a dream to occur. We can draw conclusions, if we are careful, about what consciousness a person must have, to have such a dream. I recall, when lecturing on Gilgamesh at the Club here in Zurich, Jung put that question to me: "What kind of consciousness has Gilgamesh if he has such a dream – that a star falls on him?" So it is all right, if you have a lot of experience, to do dream interpretation through comparison.

5. The Many-Faceted Ishtar

Now the best known among the lovers of Ishtar is Tammuz, the son-lover par excellence. Or Dumuzi, as he is also called. Women lament for him year after year when he dies, and he resurrects in the spring. In Ezekiel 8:14 we read: "the women sat weeping for Tammuz." The Phoenicians called him Adon, i.e. "Lord," and wept over his death. They passed this ritual on to the Greeks, who Grecized the name into Adonis. Women planted gardens for Adonis, who, with the Egyptian god Osiris, besides Tammuz, are forms of the young dying and resurrecting gods, who all belong to mother goddess religions. The Swiss semiticist Walter Baumgartner has shown that the custom of planting gardens for the resurrection of Adonis has been preserved in Sardinia to the present day. Naturally, it has switched to Jesus, but the roots of it go back to the Adonis cult. Many rituals of eastern cults have been changed into Christian rituals. In another mythological fragment, "Ishtar's Descent to the Underworld," we read how Ishtar herself fetches him out of the underworld. Tammuz's death is caused by the devouring passion of Ishtar, the great summer heat. But she brings him back from the underworld every year. During her stay there, all vegetation, all begetting and growing on earth, stops. As the veiled Ishtar, she is the bride, the life-giving Spring. As the unveiled Ishtar she has an underworld character, she brings death, and kills her lovers. She is life itself, one could say, which includes death, which belongs to the ambivalent archetype of the great mother, the life-giving and life-destroying mother. But she has other aspects besides that of mother and lover. She is also the "queen of heaven and of the stars," and leads the hosts of the stars. There are pictures of Ishtar Barbarta where she has a beard and is a warrior, hermaphroditic as it were. She has these features especially as Ishtar of Akkad, in north Babylonia, and of Nineveh and Arbela, whereas in the south, as in Uruk, she is rather the love and mother goddess. As such, for instance, she says to the Sumerian king, Gudea, about 2500 B.C.E.: "I am the holy cow who gives birth like a woman." As mother goddess she often is represented naked with a child at her breast. But with all this, her full character is still not exhausted. As the great innkeeper she has Dionysian traits. We shall meet her as such in our epic in the 10th tablet, in the figure of Siduri. The original cuneiform sign for Ishtar was a gate with a curtain of reeds which could be drawn back – the sign of a brothel. This sign was later turned into a horizontal position and was one of the ideograms for Ishtar. In the astral system she is Venus. Her emblem is a star with 8 or 16 rays. Many of these characteristics of Ishtar, her whole ambivalent fullness, can be sensed in an old prayer to her, which is known to us from the Assurbanipal library. I should like to read parts of it to you.

Thou, all mistresses' mistress, and all goddesses' goddess,
Thee I implore.
Ishtar, queen of all lands, ruler of man,
Strong art thou, an empress high.
Thy name be hallowed.
Thou art the source of light for heaven and earth,
*   thou strong daughter of Sin.*
Thou guidest the arms of the warrior,
And setteth the stage for the battle to happen.
Mistress whose splendor and greatness is beyond all the gods!
Star, thou, of the battle's tumult,
Thou who bringeth discord into the midst of brothers who lived in
*   peace and harmony before,*
Thou who betrayeth the covenant of friendship and love,
Mistress of the battlefield thou, who overturneth mountains,
Where is not thy name and thy commandments?
Thou art great, thou art splendid.
Strongest of all rulers thou, who leadeth kings by the rein like horses,
Who openeth the womb of barren women.
The men's goddess, the women's Ishtar!
Whose decisions no one can predict.

Where thou lookest, the dead become alive again, the afflicted one
                    rises from his sickbed,
And he who went astray finds the right path again, when he
                    beholds thy countenance.
Irnini, glory, and grim lion thou, may thy heart find peace.
Thou, wild bull of fury, may thy soul be pacified.
Let thine eyes rest mercifully upon me.
Thou in thy radiance, look upon me with grace.
Ishtar is great. Ishtar is queen.
The mistress is full of glory, the mistress is queen.
Irnini, daughter of Sin, thou strong one,
                    there is none equal to thee. *

Let us now hear the reaction of this mighty queen of the
gods to Gilgamesh's refusal:

6. Ishtar's Rage

When Ishtar heard this,
Ishtar burst into a rage and ascended to heaven.
Ishtar went before Anu, her father;
She went before Antum, her mother, and said:
"My father, Gilgamesh has insulted me.
Gilgamesh has enumerated my stinking deeds,
My stinking deeds and my rotten acts."
Anu opened his mouth and said,
Speaking to the great Ishtar:
"Thou thyself didst invite the ....
And so Gilgamesh enumerated thy stinking deeds,
Thy stinking deeds and thy rotten acts."
Ishtar opened her mouth and said,
Speaking to Anu, her father:

* Editor's note: the source of the above translation could not, unfortunately, be found among the author's papers. A translation by F. J. Ste-
phens, of the full text of the same prayer, can be found in ANET, pp. 384f.

"My father, create for me the bull of heaven that he may destroy Gilgamesh!"

(Tabl. VI, lines 80-94, Heidel p. 52f)

This conversation between Ishtar and her father Anu is precious from a psychological point of view. Ishtar is deeply hurt and complains to him about Gilgamesh. What do you think of her saying "He has enumerated my stinking deeds and my rotten acts"? Speiser translates here "He has recounted my stinking deeds, my stench and my foulness." What attitude in Ishtar does this show? What attitude does she have toward her behavior?

REMARKS: She does not say she did not do them.
She openly wears her very long shadow.

Picture 5: Ishtar with foot on lion

Yes, that is a very good point, and we must discriminate here. You pat her shoulder for being so conscious about her shadow, do you not? But I find it a little dangerous here, because she really has no insight. You see, if she would honestly *know* what she did, it would change something in her. Her rage would break. If she would really know 'well, after all, I really am that way, and so why should he...?' that would be a higher insight. She has not integrated it.

REMARK: That sounds like a spoiled child.

Absolutely! I understand your comment because if she would think she is so wonderful and good, that would be even worse. She sees herself, *but,* and here comes a deep problem: she has, I would say, a natural amorality. She has no conflict about being that way. She sees it, but it does not matter. One can say, 'this is my shadow,' and that is fine, it sounds perfectly enlightened, but how do we feel about it? What do we do about it? If, in the same breath, it does not make us more modest, it is only an 'I am so, and you just take it.' And she wants revenge! What does that imply? That Gilgamesh naturally should just swallow her evil deeds and rotten acts, and has no right to resist them. It has the tempting quality of pseudo-insight. It is not a full insight. How do we know this? Because it does not change her attitude. At least not toward Gilgamesh, as you will see. It is really interesting. She is unburdened of any moral conflict, which, in the deepest sense, is an inhuman situation. Jung once said: "What makes man human is to have conflict." She has a natural amorality which expresses itself in the fact that she is not enraged at Gilgamesh's reproaches, but at the fact that he dares to utter them. That is the bad thing. He was not wrong; naturally she did all this. But woe to him, he dared to tell her so! Anu tries to bring her to her senses, and to soothe her. It really sounds something like an analytic hour:

Ishtar: Create for me the bull of heaven that he may
           destroy Gilgamesh!

Anu: But please, have you not brought that onto
           yourself? Thou thyself didst invite (the insult) and
           so Gilgamesh enumerated thy stinking deeds and
           thy rotten acts.

Ishtar: My father, create for me the bull of heaven that he
           may destroy Gilgamesh.

and so on. What is the reaction to what Anu said? Zero. She does not even pick it up, as though he had not said anything. And that is naturally a typical sign of what?

REMARK: Unconsciousness.

Unconsciousness, and I would say of being possessed. By her rage – or one could even say being possessed by an animus state. She can not even listen to what the other one says. She just goes rambling on. She wants to have her bull, the bull, which is the snorting symbol of her own rage. She threatens:

> *But if thou wilt not create for me the bull of heaven,*
> *I will smash the door of the underworld and break the bolt;*
> *I will let the door stand wide open;*
> *I will cause the dead to rise that they may eat as the living*
> *So that the dead will be more numerous than the living!"*
> *Anu opened his mouth and said,*
> *Speaking to the great Ishtar:*
> *"If I do what thou desirest of me,*
> *There will be seven years of empty straw.*
> *Hast thou gathered enough grain for the people?*
> *Hast thou grown enough fodder for the cattle?"*
> *Ishtar opened her mouth and said,*
> *Speaking to Anu, her father:*
> *"I have heaped up grain for the people,*
> *I have grown fodder for the cattle.*

If there will be seven years of empty straw,
I have gathered enough grain for the people,
And I have grown enough fodder for the cattle."

(Tabl. VI, lines 96-113, Heidel p.53)

And her threats are plenty and powerful. Her threats, in the event that he would not give in, show her in her full power. She is able to bring the dead to life again, so that they may eat with the living. So she can destroy the whole creation. The destructive power of a possessed state could not be more clearly shown than here. It could seem as though Anu is weak and gives in. But I think he is wise. He chooses the lesser evil. He grants her the heavenly bull, but he makes certain conditions. She is mightier than he. He has to give in. But he guarantees, somehow. He makes a compromise with her. OK, have your heavenly bull. Let him loose on Gilgamesh. But do not destroy creation. Provide. Here you can see that she is also a vegetation goddess. She is really the mistress over life and death. If she wants, the grain will grow, and if she does not want, there will be drought. I think it is clear that Anu does not give in out of sheer weakness, but out of wisdom, for he causes Ishtar to make this provision for mankind, since releasing the heavenly bull brings about seven lean years. You may recognize in this a motif similar to that appearing in the Biblical story of Joseph and the Pharaoh's dream of the seven fat and seven lean kine, representing seven fat years and seven lean years. Now the bull is described in the following as a snorting monster.

7. Facing the Bull of Heaven

The bull of heaven descended....
With his first snort he killed a hundred men.
Two hundred men. ... three hundred men.
With his second snort he killed a hundred.... in addition (?)
Two hundred men ... in addition (?)... three hundred men.

.... in addition(?).
With his third snort he rushed at Enkidu,
But Enkidu dodged his attack.
Enkidu leaped and seized the bull of heaven by his horns.
The bull of heaven threw foam at his face.
He touched him with the thick of his tail....
Enkidu opened his mouth and said,
Speaking to Gilgamesh
"My friend, we boasted....

and then there is a gap. He probably said 'we were too fast, we thought we could make it too easily.' It's a very mutilated text in which we can only understand that finally they did make it.

And between the nape and his horns....
....
Enkidu chased him and ... the bull of heaven
He seized him by the thick of his tail ...
....
Between the nape and the horns he thrust his sword....
When they had killed the bull of heaven, they tore out his heart
And placed it before Shamash.
They stepped back and prostrated themselves before Shamash.
(Tabl. VI, lines 122-155, Heidel p. 53f)

In the prayer to Ishtar we just read, she is called 'a raging wild bull.' So the bull, seen from Ishtar's side, is the hypostasis, so to speak, of her own raging wrath. Its killing power, "with one snort," was similarly described earlier as the fire coming out of the mouth of Humbaba. He too had this fiery destructive quality. So there is a connection between Humbaba and the bull. We have seen that Humbaba was the guardian of Ishtar's holy forest. Here this bull is her own rage, psychologically spoken, whose breath, like Humbaba's, brought death. But whereas Humbaba was hidden in the cedar forest, in other words, in the unconscious, where

Pictures 6 and 7: The Fight with the Bull of Heaven

Gilgamesh and Enkidu had to go to find him, the bull comes into the center of Uruk, and he is the aggressive one. There is a difference of situation, with a corresponding difference in psychological meaning. It is not a matter of the heroes' going into the forest to find a so to speak unprepared Humbaba. What is Uruk, the city? It is his own city. It is his consciousness. It is a breakthrough of an unconscious affect into the realm of consciousness. I do not know how much they are aware, but they are in a better position. That something breaks through can happen to us any time, but if such an affect becomes conscious, enters the center of consciousness, it is vastly different than if it is totally unconscious. If it becomes conscious, one has the possibility of grasping it by the horns, as is done here.

REMARK: It also indicates the progression of libido, in that it approaches consciousness; in the other way consciousness was seeking or regressing to Humbaba.

Yes, there is something in what you say, but I would not make the discrimination quite like that. I would say that Gilgamesh had an intuition that there is this Humbaba, and he goes as it were into the unconscious to meet the "perils of the soul," as in the night sea journey. It is a kind of night sea journey. Whilst here, in his own city, he has his friends around him in a different way. We need all our consciousness to be up to a break-in of the unconscious. He is also in a better position because he has fought Humbaba already. And happening in his own reality, he is better able to grasp it, as he and Enkidu do here. Which does not always mean that one can overcome it. To do so is the heroic privilege. It needs the help of the Self to be able to deal with such an inner power. There is another thing which is important here. By creating this bull of heaven, or asking Anu to create it, and getting it into her power, and letting it attack Gilgamesh, Ishtar has given herself away, by her very wrath. She is no longer behind the screen. *In* the bull, she breaks into consciousness, and is attackable, so to speak. The unconscious content represented by the heavenly bull is thus much closer to consciousness – that is what it amounts to. It even penetrates consciousness, and therefore can be grasped. But we must remember that Gilgamesh himself has been called a wild ox, in the first tablet: "Aruru brought this furious wild ox into being." And in the fight between Gilgamesh and Enkidu, they were both compared with bulls. This is a general Babylonian trait. Hammurabi, and later on, the Assyrian kings, liked to give themselves the epithet of 'wild bull.' Hunting of bulls was a much prized sport of the Babylonian kings. Psychologically, this episode seems to me to allude to the fact that Gilgamesh and Enkidu, in fighting against the heavenly bull of Ishtar, fight against this bull nature in themselves. For what would this bull nature be? Psychologically, the bull really belongs to Ishtar. It is her primitive raging affective masculine side. Now if Gilgamesh and Enkidu fight this bull, they are engaged with the image of Ishtar. Since they themselves are bulls, fighting this bull means that they are fighting the danger of *embodying the animus of the mother.*

The danger of sons identifying with the animus of the mother is evident in those who "choose" the profession of the mother's choice. If the mother does not develop her animus, it will be projected onto the precious son who has to do all that she really would want to do. There are cases of outspoken unconscious identity where the son enters a profession he never really started to want and to decide on, by himself. It was just self-evident that this was for him. This is often actually acting out the mother's unconscious animus projection, or sometimes not so unconscious on her part, in that she "knows" what is good for him. Where the son is not unconsciously acting out the mother's projection, it can also be positive, his achievements having some ambitions of the mother behind them. Another kind of identification with the mother's animus is to be seen in a kind of primitive he-man persona which is not a real masculinity. It is a display of a rough aggressiveness which is a built-up reproduction of a certain animus quality, and it is all the mother. That is sometimes very difficult to discriminate in the analytical process. To come back to our heroes:

When they had killed the bull of heaven, they tore out his heart
And placed it before Shamash.
They stepped back and prostrated themselves before Shamash.
(Tabl. VI, lines 153-155, Heidel p. 54)

In other words, they sacrifice the heart of the bull to Shamash. And what is the heart? In a figurative sense it is the center, the essence. The bull they have to kill stands for Ishtar, and they sacrifice the essence of what this bull represents. They sacrifice it to Shamash. Shamash is really the counter-pole to Ishtar. Yes, one could say that Shamash is the masculine Self, but one could also say he is the spiritual element. They sacrifice that bull nature which they overcome, coming from the mother, and bring it to Shamash, the patron god of Gilgamesh, the sun god, standing for a higher consciousness. We can see in this whole symbolism a transitus from the realm of the mother to the realm of the father. This is what makes the Gilgamesh epic, beyond itself, very important from the point of view of religious history. It is namely a transitus to a new religious era, which leads, for instance, into the monotheism in the Old Testament. We find that in a number of spots of the epic, as we will see. They sacrifice, so to speak, their own bull nature, which corresponds to an identity with the mother animus, to a new development of consciousness, to Shamash. There is another interesting aspect to this symbolism: the bull is the zodiacal sign of Venus (=Ishtar), and astrologically it indicates the fertility of the earth. This can also be seen in our text. The fact that the bull of heaven was given to Ishtar caused vegetation to stop functioning. Astrologically the sign of the ram follows that of the bull. The ram is a fiery sign, and according to astrologists, it symbolizes the time of the Old Testament, which was led over to by the sun gods, Shamash and Marduk.

After the overcoming of the heavenly bull, Ishtar climbs up onto the wall of Uruk and curses Gilgamesh:

> *Woe unto Gilgamesh, who has besmirched me and has killed*
> *the bull of heaven!*
> *When Enkidu heard this speech of Ishtar,*
> *He tore out the right thigh of the bull of heaven*
> *and tossed it before her, saying:*
> *"If only I could get hold of thee,*
> *I would do unto thee as unto him;*
> *Or I would tie his entrails to thy side!"*
>
> (Tabl. VI, lines 159-164, Heidel p. 54)

Jensen, one of the early translators of the Gilgamesh Epic, identifies Gilgamesh and Enkidu with the Gemini in the Zodiac, and called attention to the fact that in the chart of the stars the bull rushes at the twins with lowered horns. He connects the torn-out thigh with missing hindquarter of the bull in the star constellation. The word is mutilated in the text. In the translations it is rendered as "the right thigh." Gressmann mentions that the thigh is perhaps a euphemism for the phallus. This does not sound unlikely to me. In that case, the phallus of the bull would represent a sort of malicious surrogate for Gilgamesh's love. There is a similar example: Astarte persecutes her lover, the Phoenician god Edmun, at the chase. He dismembers himself. Had Gilgamesh given in to Ishtar, it would also have meant a self-castration. But as it is, this falls back on Ishtar herself. It happens to her bull, so to speak. The nearest parallel is perhaps the Phrygian story of Zeus, who tears out the testicles of a ram and throws them publicly into the lap of Deo, a name for Cybele, another name for the mother goddess. It is a defiance of castration as a symbol of the mother cult, because there was a ritual of castration in honor of the mother goddess. And this is a kind of defiance of this ritual.

As to the bowels which Enkidu wants to hang on to Ishtar,
Gressmann mentions a German cult, Hangazyr, where the
bowels of a still living sacrificed animal were wound around
the holy tree. This parallel again stresses the mother aspect
of Ishtar, if we think of the cedar. Then we read:

> *Ishtar assembled the girl-devotees,*
> *The prostitutes, and the courtesans;*
> *Over the right thigh of the bull of heaven she set up a lamentation.*
> (Tabl. VI, lines 165-167, Heidel p. 54f)

Picture 8: Enkidu

8. Homecoming of the Heroes

Here Ishtar is conquered. We hear no more of her until the eleventh tablet, where she appears in connection with the flood story which Utnapishtim tells to Gilgamesh, where we shall have to deal with her again. But now Gilgamesh and Enkidu are the praised heroes in Uruk. Gilgamesh had taken with him the horns of the heavenly bull as trophies. He hung them up in his bedroom, not unlike many young people today. They each were made of thirty pounds of lapis lazuli. The tremendous amount of oil they could contain he presented to "his tutelary god, Lugulbanda," who was his ancestor as we recall from the ancient Sumerian king list. The text says of the two heroes:

In the Euphrates they washed their hands.

(line 176, Heidel p. 55)

This may be a ritual too, a *rite de sortie,* to get them out of a fighting state after they return from their battles, as is the case with many primitive tribes too. It is not proven, but it might quite likely be a ritual to bring them back to a normal life-style. But, as we will see, the ritual was not enough to get them out of the state of feeling their victorious hero-status. On their way back to the palace, riding through the streets where the people had gathered to see them, Gilgamesh says to the maids of Uruk:

"Who is the most glorious among heroes!
Who is the most eminent among men?"

(lines 182-183, Heidel p. 55)

And the maids of Uruk answer most enthusiastically:

"Gilgamesh is the most glorious among heroes!
Gilgamesh is the most eminent among men!"

(lines 184-185, Heidel p. 55)

This recalls the well-known Old Testament passage in 1 Sam. 18:6,7:

> ... when David returned from the slaughter of the Philistine, that the women came out of all the cities of Israel, singing and dancing, to meet king Saul, with timbrels, with joy, and with three-stringed instruments, and the women sang one to another in their play, and said:
>> Saul hath slain his thousands,
>> And David his ten thousands.

It is the women who give this praise to the hero. It is the women who give Gilgamesh this wonderful inflation.

9. The Problem of Death

Back in his palace Gilgamesh celebrates with a joyful feast, after which the heroes go to sleep. But already the same night, the fall comes. A dream announces to Enkidu that the gods had decided on his death. Here something new begins: the problem of death and immortality opens. The hero Gilgamesh, the prototype of consciousness, freed from the mother, is faced with a new, specifically spiritual task. One could say a new pilgrimage begins for the soul of mankind represented in this anthropos Gilgamesh, in its process of development.

I would like to point out that we are here at the end of the sixth tablet of the epic, that is, half way through. One could say that psychologically it is also the natural break between what we could call the two parts of the epic. When the great archetype of the mother is decisively dealt with, something new opens. With Enkidu's imminent death, Gilgamesh suddenly realizes that one has to die, that life does not go on forever. To quote Jung again: in the discussion following my lecture on the Gilgamesh Epic, he said that the young man not freed from the mother lives in an eternal *status nascendi,* an eternal state of becoming. Time has no value; it goes on. That is the *puer aeternus*. He feels eternally a boy. Time does not count, life is not limited. One can live as an eternal promise of what, sometime, some day, one will be. It never comes into reality. I have seen, working with young men, that sometimes at this stage the problem of time is raised pointedly by the dreams. I remember especially one case where the dreamer was back in the school yard where a *huge* clock, not there in reality, gave the time. Now time started to count. One could not say mañana, I will do it tomorrow. It counted that one lives one's life and fulfills one's life. One could not unconsciously, irresponsibly, just go on and on, being taken care of by mother-life, not having to shoulder one's own responsibility. Therefore I find a deep meaning in the fact that the problem of death, and the related problem of immortality, starts only at a certain point, namely, when this ambivalently blissful existence in the womb of the great mother in present life, is broken.

Now Gilgamesh is open for the second task, for the quest for a meaningful life. That is what it boils down to when death counts: what does our life mean if we have to die? And is there any going on? But this is only an anticipation of the second part of the epic, which we enter now. And I want you to know that this is not a hiatus made in the epic itself, only that it seems to me to naturally lend itself here from a psychological point of view. Here I think the comparison with dreams helps to understand the myth, just as the myth is invaluable to us in understanding dreams. After the feast, which is the climax of his accomplished heroic task, Gilgamesh has to make a descent which leads him into the depths of death. But this descent changes into a different, a specifically spiritual dimension, into an ascent of Gilgamesh, whom we recognize to be the prototype of consciousness freed from the mother. It is like in Faust, where Mephisto says to him to "Go down now to the Mothers. I could also say ascend." It is a new night sea journey which starts, with another goal. After their joyful feast, the heroes go to sleep and Enkidu has a dream which he relates to Gilgamesh:

> *"My friend, why did the great gods take counsel together?*
> *My friend, hear what a dream I had last night.*
> *Anu, Enlil, Ea, and the heavenly Shamash took counsel together.*

(Anu we recall is the god of heaven, Enlil is the god of earth and storm and wind, Ea is the god of water, and Shamash we know, is the sun god.)

> *And Anu said to Enlil:*
> *'Because they have killed the bull of heaven and have killed*
>   *Huwawa*
> *That one of the two shall die,' said Anu,*
> *'Who stripped the mountains of the cedar!'*
> *But Enlil said: 'Enkidu shall die;*
> *Gilgamesh shall not die!'*
> *Now the heavenly Shamash replied to Enlil, the hero:*
> *'Have they not killed the bull of heaven and Huwawa*
>   *at my command*

(Here it comes out very clearly that Shamash, the symbol of new consciousness, was the instigator of these events.)

> *And now the innocent Enkidu shall die?'*
> *But Enlil was enraged*
> *At the heavenly Shamash and said:*
> *'Because daily thou descendest to them*
>   *as though thou wert one of their own!'"*
> (Tabl. VI, line 194, Tabl. VII, col. i, lines 3-16, Heidel p. 55f)

This reproach by the gods against another god is awfully interesting. "You mix too much with those human ones. We do not like that." The council of the gods gives us a vivid picture of a conflict in the heavenly sphere. The sacrilegious killing of Humbaba and of the heavenly bull shall be revenged. Anu demands that Gilgamesh be punished for it, especially because he has torn the cedar out of the mountain. Thus, in the divine sight, this first deed of Gilgamesh appears to be the most serious crime. In this we have it validated that this cedar is not just a cedar. It is an insult to something divine. It is an insult to Ishtar. Insofar as it signifies a symbolic killing of the mother, it is indeed the most important act, which includes the other as its consequence. Enlil pleads for Enkidu's death: "Enkidu shall die, but Gilgamesh shall not die." Only Shamash defends both of them: "Have they not killed the bull of heaven and Huwawa at my command? And now the innocent Enkidu shall die?" It should be mentioned that the text has "thy command," not "my command." But I should like to join the opinion of Schott and Heidel who think that it is pretty certainly a misunderstanding, or intentional change by the Hittite scribe, because he knows from what had been said earlier that it was Shamash who sent Gilgamesh on his way. It is also not likely, as Schott points out, that Enlil, who was the guardian of Humbaba, should have caused his death. It is clearly a mistake. At a later time there may have been a resistance to a guilt in Shamash, the sun god, the later judge of the gods. We find such "corrections" caused by resistances of a theological nature also in the Old Testament. So I think we can go along with most translators, taking it for granted that Shamash really said "at my command," because it does seem so from the whole connection. This passage, which, incidentally, is a filler-in from a Hittite rescension (wherefore also the name Huwawa instead of Humbaba) is very important in our connection, since Shamash himself declares himself to be the instigator of the heroic deeds of Gilgamesh and Enkidu. He is now really the Self-figure of the two.

Enlil's response to Shamash is especially significant in another connection. He says, full of rage, "Because daily thou descendest to them as though thou wert one of their own!" i.e., 'their equal.' So one god reproaches another for making too close a contact with mortals. Within the complexity of the divine essence, which we see here still represented as a polytheistic plurality of God, if we take them as one, there are different aspects of the divinity. Shamash, as Dr. Jung said once in a discussion of this material, is the mystery of consciousness, the archetype of consciousness in the unconscious, in the realm of the gods. And that is what the other gods, who want to remain in their divine unconsciousness, do not like. This same quarrel between the gods you also find in the Old Testament, but in another form; namely in the ambivalence of Yahweh, the divine God personality, Who fosters, and at the same time rejects, the idea that human beings should become conscious; Who, in Genesis 6, in "the sons of God," unites with the daughters of man, and Who nevertheless punishes both of them for it. The idea is this: that in what is still seen as separate aspects, as in our Epic, we have a conflict between different gods in the pantheon, in the 'family,' which Dr. Marie-Louise von Franz very nicely called "the archetypes at home." With the archetypes at home, we have a domestic fight. One could say, from the phenomenology of the Old Testament, that this quarrel is seen in another situation, or is situated differently, namely within one divine ambivalent soul, which has different aspects. For instance, in the Genesis story, God says: "Do not eat from this tree!" The snake comes and says: "You go ahead and eat, and then you will become like God." This is a divine impulse, psychologically seen, to counteract the wish that man should not become conscious. Because afterwards the whole plan of salvation is built up on the fact that man *does* have this consciousness to discriminate between good and evil. We can see in the very old text of Genesis 6, where the sons of God unite with the humans, that these sons of God, the *Benai HaElohim,* belong to the divine court. They are divine substance. They are aspects of the divine, of Yahweh. That goes deep into the question, which you can read in my book *Satan in the Old Testament,* for Satan is also one of the *Benai HaElohim.* There I show more elaborately how even the right translation of *Benai HaElohim* means parts, or aspects, of God; individuals of the divine substance. And they unite with the daughters of man, and are punished for it, so there is also a contradiction, two different impulses. There it is a conflict between two sides of Yahweh. In our Epic, it is between Shamash and Enlil. This is not the only case. There are even words, as we will later see, which Ishtar says, which Yahweh also says. Such comparisons give a unique insight into the dynamics of religious symbolism.

VI

THE IMPACT OF DEATH

1. Enkidu's Illness

The offended Enlil seems to gain the victory in the council of the gods, because after this dream Enkidu falls ill. Gilgamesh weeps streams of tears and says:

> *"My brother, my dear brother, why do they acquit me instead of thee?"*
> *Moreover he said: "Shall I sit down by the spirit of the dead,*
> *At the door of the spirit of the dead?*
> *And shall I never again see my dear brother with mine eyes?"*
> (Tabl. VII, col. i, lines 19-22, Heidel p. 57)

His first reaction, as you can see, is a feeling that the gods have done an injustice in not condemning him, but Enkidu in his place. He realizes that Enkidu will be sacrificed in his stead. But he only raises his painful question to the gods and leaves it open as a question, as though he would sense that what is going to happen will be tragic and meaningful at the same time. The gods are not just, but they create meaning, which in the best case, may be equal to a higher justice. What happens to Enkidu may be compared to the fate of Esau, the firstborn son, who should get his father's blessing according to an old custom. But he is rejected in favor of Jacob, because Jacob is the bearer of salvation, i.e., the bearer of a new spiritual development, and is therefore placed above his elder but more primitive brother. This event (Genesis 27), which is unjust and meaningful at the same time, is brought about by God's intent, and Rebekah herself, the mother of the twins, is God's accomplice. After Gilgamesh has realized what was happening, his purely personal and simply human reaction occurs. He suffers anxiety and pain over the impending loss of his dear comrade.

Enkidu himself, this animal-like natural man, raised from the mother realm, who was lured into the world of culture, suffers, during his illness, an outbreak of pent-up resentments against the world of culture. In a typically primitive way, he first curses the gate of the cedar forest which by its beauty lured him to enter the forest. It was then, as you may remember, that his tragic fate was first forecast by the paralysis of his hand. Then he calls down the curse of Shamash on the hunter, and last, he curses the hierodule:

> *"Come, O prostitute, thy destiny I will decree,*
> *A destiny that shall not end for all eternity.*
> *I will curse thee with a mighty curse.*
> *.... may its curses rise up early against thee.*
> ... [9 lines too fragmentary for translation]....
> *.... the street shall be thy dwelling place.*
> *The shade of the wall shall be thine abode.*
> *.... thy feet.*
> *May the drunken and the thirsty alike smite thy cheek."*
>
> (Tabl. VII, col. iii, lines 6-22, Heidel p. 58)

When Shamash hears that, he calls him from heaven:

> *"Why, O Enkidu, dost thou curse the courtesan, the prostitute,*
> *Who taught thee to eat bread fit for divinity,*
> *To drink wine fit for royalty,*
> *Who clothed thee with a magnificent garment,*
> *And who gave thee splendid Gilgamesh for thy companion?"*
>
> (lines 35-39, Heidel p. 59)

and he goes on to describe how Gilgamesh shows him great

honor, and how deeply he will mourn him when he dies. "When Enkidu heard the words of valiant Shamash," the text continues, "his angry heart grew quiet." Quite willingly he now begins to bless the hierodule whom before he had cursed:

> *Kings, princes, and grandees shall love thee.*
> *.... the ... shall unloose his girdle for thee.*
> *.... basalt, lapis lazuli, and gold.*
> *For thee.... his storehouses are filled.*
> *Before the gods the priest shall lead thee.*
> *On account of thee the wife, the mother of seven, shall be forsaken."*
>   (Tabl. VII, col. iv, lines 2-10, Heidel p. 59f)

From this sudden change of mind in Enkidu we can tell that he has not really been affected in his depth by Shamash, and that he has only been drawn along on the heroic path. He is obeying Shamash, but he is not really convinced deep down. The text goes on:

> *.... Enkidu, whose body is sick.*
> *.... he sleeps alone.*
> *.... during the night he pours out his heart to his friend.*
> *"My friend, I saw a dream this night.*
> *The heavens roared, the earth resounded.*
> *.... I was standing by myself.*
> *.... appeared, somber was his face.*
> *His face was like that of Zu.*
> *.... his talons were like the talons of an eagle.*
> *.... he overpowered me.*
> *.... he leaps.*
> *.... submerged me.*
> ....[break of 9 lines]
> *.... he transformed me,*
> *That mine arms were covered with feathers like a bird.*
> *He looks at me and leads me to the house of darkness,*
>   *to the dwelling of Irkalla;*

To the house from which he who enters never goes forth;
On the road whose path does not lead back;
To the house whose occupants are bereft of light;
Where dust is their food and clay their sustenance;
Where they are clad like birds, with garments of wings;
Where they see no light and dwell in darkness.
In the house of dust, which I entered,
. . . .
There also dwells Ereshkigal, queen of the underworld.
Bêlit-sêri, the lady scribe of the underworld, squats before her.
She holds a tablet and reads before her.
She lifted her head and saw me.
She said: 'Who has brought this man here?'"

(Tabl. VII, col. iv, lines 11-54, Heidel p. 60f)

We have here a description of the Babylonian nether
world. Enkidu, tragically sacrificed for the sake of his friend's
sun-like way to consciousness, unable to understand why he
has to die, receives in this dream again a confirmation of the
unchangeable verdict of the gods. In the dream a bird-man
with a dark face leads him into the netherworld, and Bêlit-
sêri, the female scribe of the underworld, then actually
receives him into the realm of the dead. The man with the
face of a bird may be a demon of the underworld, fetching
men down and changing them, as we have just heard, into
feathered birds.

2. The Land of the Dead

In order to feel the full impact of the shock which Gilgamesh is going to experience, and in order to understand his
desperate search for immortality, we have to conjure up the
image of the netherworld, i.e., the Babylonian concept of
life after death. To the old Babylonians, death is the "inescapable nightly destiny" which puts an end to all human
brightness, according to 'age-old laws.' All their prayers call

for a long life, for immortality on earth through descendants. A prayer by Nebuchadnezzar has the following text: "Durable like the bricks of Ibarra make my years, extend them into eternity." The Babylonian netherworld is not a different new life. It is only the reversal of life on earth. It is endlessly sad and dark, without any change. It is the shadow life. We know about it not only from the Gilgamesh Epic, but also from other mythological fragments, especially from the story of Nergal and Ereshkigal, god and goddess of the underworld, and also from "Ishtar's Journey to the Underworld." Still other descriptions have been gathered and published. You find quite a bit about these conceptions in the commentaries, also in Heidel, although his ideas concerning the Old Testament concept about life after death are not convincing, and are not really accepted in the literature. From those fragments we learn that the spirit of the dead person enters into the underworld by 14 or 7 portals. There the guardians treat him "according to the old law." The underworld is also called, as we saw in Enkidu's dream, "the land without return," or "the land of the dead," or "the far away land." It was thought to lie in the west, which to the old Babylonians also meant the desert, a frightening place where demons live. The identity of underworld and desert, is evidenced by the fact that Bêlit-sêri, the scribe of the netherworld, whom we met at the end of the dream of Enkidu, is also a goddess of the desert. Furthermore, Ereshkigal, the goddess of the underworld, was imagined as a monster with a lion's head. She has snakes in her hands, and animals suck at her breasts. Her husband Nergal, too, is a lion god. It is Ereshkigal who watches over "the old laws" of the underworld. You can see here again, as with the heavenly gods, that the feminine principle is the stronger one, for Nergal is but the prince consort. This myth yields so much information in connection with our theme that I would like to go into it briefly. The myth tells that Nergal first belonged to the heavenly gods before he descended to the underworld and became the husband of Ereshkigal. How this came about we learn from the following.

The gods in the underworld told Ereshkigal to send a messenger up to heaven to get food from there. So they seem to have had a community kitchen up there for all the gods. Ereshkigal dispatched a messenger, and when he entered heaven all the gods rose to greet him; all, that is, but Nergal. When the messenger returned and told Ershkigal what had happened, she became so furious that she sent him back to heaven to fetch this disrespectful Nergal; in today's language, to extradite him. She said: "The god who did not get up in the presence of my messenger – bring him here so that I may kill him!" Does this not sound familiar? It is not difficult to discover behind this outbreak of temper – to put it mildly – Ishtar's demand for power, whose underworld aspect is, as it were, Ereshkigal. Ereshkigal is really a kind of sister of Ishtar. Just recall Ishtar's threat before Anu when she wanted him to create for her the heavenly bull, that if he would not she would "cause the dead to rise that they may ... be more numerous than the living!" There you can see that she has power over the underworld too, and one can only say that that aspect of her is, psychologically spoken, Ereshkigal. So the messenger went back in order to convey Ereshkigal's claim for extradition, and, believe it or not, the gods did not dare to resist. They really handed Nergal over. But when he arrived in the underworld, he approached Ereshkigal in wild determination, tore her down from her throne and threatened to cut off her head. Then she began to cry and lament and – made him a marriage proposal! Whereupon he kissed her, wiped her tears away, and said: "Whatever you wanted to get from me all these months, you shall have!" And so it came about that Nergal, formerly a heavenly god, became a god of the underworld, but nevertheless subservient to Ereshkigal. Ereshkigal was stronger than Nergal, and in the end the feminine principle was triumphant here in contrast to Ishtar's unsuccessful wooing of Gilgamesh. On this background, of the wooing goddess, you can see again the epochal change of pattern in Gilgamesh's resisting Ishtar.

Now let us go on with the description of the Babylonian underworld. When the spirit of the dead person enters, the guardian gives his name to Ereshkigal. If she is angry at him, she curses him with the so-called great curse. With the help of the Annunaki, the seven dreaded judges of the nether-world, she jealously guards the source of life which is to be found, as I mentioned earlier, in the underworld; for if the dead could reach it they would be able to liberate themselves from Ereshkigal's power. This, in my opinion, indicates that with the old Babylonians *to be dead meant to be in the power of the dark, the devouring mother.* It is worthwhile in this connection to turn our attention for a moment to the question: what concept of life after death is to be found in the Old Testament? The comparison is very interesting.

In the Old Testament we also find a concept of the underworld, the She'ol, but it is rather colorless, and appears only on the periphery, as it were. Here too, we find the ideal of a long earthly life, after which nothing occurs that would deserve the name of life. And equally, in the Old Testament we have not yet an idea of the immortality of the soul. However, the concept of She'ol is charged with very little libido in contrast to the Babylonian conception of the un-derworld. How can we explain this? It seems to be connect-ed with the fact that in the Old Testament life on earth is so much bound up with God and dedicated to Him, that a life in the hereafter is, as it were, already taken into the earthly life. And from here a line of development leads to the concept of the immortal soul which shines through in a number of passages of the Old Testament, especially in the so-called Songs of the suffering Servant of God in Isaiah 53, and also in Job 19:25ff.

As for the etymology of She'ol: formerly it was thought to come from the root *sha'al*, which means to ask, to claim; *Orcus rapax* (the greedy underworld), so to speak, but today one thinks that the word means depth, or cavity. Perhaps it was even an old proper name of an underworld deity, for it always appears without the article. To 'go down to She'ol' is an idiomatic expression in the Old Testament which we find, for example, in Gen. 37:35 where Jacob, believing his son Joseph to have been devoured by a wild animal, says: "...I will go down to the grave (literally She'ol) to my son, mourning." In Isaiah 38:10 we find "the *gates* of the netherworld (She'ol)" mentioned. Especially valuable in connection with our theme is Isaiah 5:14, because She'ol there is really described as a devouring monster: "Therefore hell (She'ol) hath enlarged herself, and opened her mouth without measure..."

Returning to the epic: against this background of the conventional Babylonian concept of life after death, its hopelessness and despair, we have to realize that it is Enkidu's fate to be taken down into that underworld. He is the primitive nature-bound human creature; his is the way of nature. For the instinctive nature-bound primitive man, that is his way. But as we have already seen in the dream of the toppling mountain, and as we will also see later on, Gilgamesh is going to be changed by Enkidu's life *and* death, and will be prepared for another life, for a spiritual life. I would like to remark here that in all the commentaries you will find it said that Gilgamesh was a very ambitious man, and that he wanted immortality, and that the only change which happened to him was that he had to submit to the fact that he had to die. He comes back to Uruk and recalls his building up its walls again, and that's that. This is not wrong. It also needs a change of attitude, which he had, because he wanted to storm the heavens, so to speak. He wanted to be the one who would not die, understood in the sense of living eternally. Not another life, but a continuation of this life, a wish which every natural being has. But I feel, to anticipate a little, that this change does not mean that he has not gotten any new spiritual life. It *belongs* to the spiritual life that he must first accept death. Because if he hangs on to natural life nothing else can open. On Jung's gravestone in Küsnacht is the inscription (which he himself chose for the family plot): *"Primus homo de terra terranus; secundus homo de coelo coelestis."* (The first man is from the earth, he is earthy; the second man is from heaven, he is heavenly.) I mention this because, if we take over these terms of *primus homo* and *secundus homo,* I would say that Gilgamesh enters somewhat into a dawning, an inner knowledge of *secundus homo.* But he had to finish with the *primus homo* first, otherwise the *secundus homo de coelo* can not get into being at all. If one just hangs on to life, and immortality means only not dying, then the *secundus homo* is not yet born. That is usually a matter of the second half of life, and we will be able to see that *this* journey is really a journey of the second half of life. Which does not mean that it is a matter merely of years. *When* people are called to the problem of the second half of life is a matter of fate. Enkidu loses his life. He remained buried under the toppling mountain. But through his life and death, Gilgamesh gains the light experience which helps him to find a life beyond the nature cycle of the life-giving and life-taking mother.

3. The Mourning of Gilgamesh

After his ominous dream Enkidu gets steadily worse. Before death comes to him, he complains to Gilgamesh that he cannot even die as a warrior on the battlefield. This was regarded as the most honorable death, and, as we can see in the 12th tablet of the epic, the warrior who died in battle had a somewhat easier lot, since his father and mother could support his head. At the beginning of the 8th tablet we find Gilgamesh at dawn at Enkidu's death bed.

As soon as the first shimmer of morning beamed forth,
Gilgamesh said to his friend:
"O Enkidu, my friend, to whom the gazelle was mother
And the wild ass was father,

It was thou whom the.... reared.
And.... the pasture.
Mountains we ascended and went down to the cedar forest.
                    (Tabl. VIII, col. i, lines 1-7, Heidel p. 62)

After a large gap, in which he seems to have called on the animals of the steppe to mourn for Enkidu, we find him expressing his deep grief over his loss before the elders of Uruk. In retrospect he experiences again their whole life together, and realizes what Enkidu meant for him.

Hearken unto me, O elders, and give ear unto me!
It is for Enkidu, my friend, that I weep,
Crying bitterly like unto a wailing woman.
The hatchet at my side, the trusty weapon of my arm,
The dagger in my belt, the shield that was before me,
My festal attire, my only joy!
An evil foe arose and robbed me.
My friend, my younger brother, who chased the wild ass of the open
                    country and the panther of the steppe;
Enkidu, my friend, my younger brother, who chased the wild ass of
                    the open country and the panther of the steppe;
                    (Tabl. VIII, col. ii, lines 1-9, Heidel p. 62f)

You see here again the style of repetition which makes it especially impressive. He will repeat these same words later to Siduri, to Utnapishtim, to Urshanabi, the boatman of Utnapishtim, and so on. This archaic style of repetition is held to indicate that the epic was originally orally transmitted, not written.

We who conquered all the difficulties, who ascended the mountains;
Who seized and killed the bull of heaven;
Who overthrew Hubaba, that dwelt in the cedar forest – !
Now what means this sleep which has taken hold of thee?
Thou hast become dark and canst not hear me."
And indeed he does not lift his eyes.

He touched his heart, but it did not beat.
Then he veiled his friend like a bride....
He lifted his voice like a lion,
Like a lioness robbed of her whelps.
Again and again he turned to his friend,
Pulling out his hair and throwing it away....
Taking off and throwing down his beautiful clothes....

(lines 10-22, Heidel p. 63)

All this oriental expression of grief. Unfortunately the rest of the 8th tablet has still more gaps, so we can only surmise what happens. Gilgamesh performs a ritual of mourning which Shamash had already described to Enkidu when the latter cursed the hierodule, etc., in his resentment at having been seduced into culture. Shamash quieted him then with his recital of the honors Gilgamesh gives him, and foretold what Gilgamesh himself now says, repeating Shamash verbatim.

On a couch of honor I let thee recline.
I let thee sit on a seat of ease, the seat at my left,
So that the princes of the earth kissed thy feet.
Over thee I will cause the people of Uruk to weep and to lament
The thriving people I will burden with service for thee.
And I myself, after thou art buried, will cause my body to wear
                              long hair.
I will clothe myself with the skin of a lion and will roam over the
                              desert."

(Tabl. VIII, col. iii, lines 1-7, Heidel p. 63f)

Schott, the German translator of the Gilgamesh Epic, assumes that Gilgamesh was hoping to call Enkidu back to life by his lamentation, and that therefore he delayed the burial. This is confirmed by the 10th tablet where Gilgamesh says to Utnapishtim about Enkidu: "For burial I did not want to give him up, Until the worm fell upon his face." So he did not want to bury him, hoping to keep him alive. But then he starts to perform the rituals of the burial:

> *As soon as the first shimmer of morning beamed forth, Gilgamesh*
> *fashioned....*
> *He brought out a large table of elammaqu-wood.*
> *A bowl of carnelian he filled with honey.*
> *A bowl of lapis lazuli he filled with butter.*
> *.... he adorned and exposed to the sun.*
>
> (Tabl. VIII, col. v, lines 45-49, Heidel p. 64)

It is known that in old Babylonia the bodies of the dead were embalmed with butter, honey, oil and salt, wrapped in linen, covered with aromatic spices, and placed on a bier of stone. Wailing women and men accompanied the burial procession playing flutes, and the relatives of the deceased wore hair shirts. The mourning itself was very expressive. In the annals of King Sargon we read about a mourning Babylonian: "He sat on the earth, tore his clothes, took a knife to wound himself, and burst into tears." The mourning lasted seven days. Some of these practices in reduced form, such as sitting on the floor or on a low stool or box during seven days of mourning, and to make a tear in ones clothes, have remained as Jewish mourning rituals to the present day. The dead were always buried, not cremated. To be cremated after death was considered a disgrace. We can find this also in the Old Testament, in Amos 2:1, where Moab was faulted for burning the remains of an Edomite king.

In tablet 9 we read again that Gilgamesh is mourning:

> *Gilgamesh for Enkidu, his friend,*
> *Weeps bitterly and roams over the desert.*
> *"When I die, shall I not be like unto Enkidu?*
> *Sorrow has entered my heart.*
> *I am afraid of death and roam over the desert."*
>
> (Tabl. IX, col. i, lines 1-5, Heidel p. 64)

What can we see in this threefold mention of mourning?

In the first, he mourns the loss of the friend, and recalls all the things they had done together. In the next, he performs all these rituals. That is, after the personal mourning for the lost friend, came the execution of the collective rites. One could say, 'that is enough.' What does this further manifestation signify? Psychologically? When he says: "When I die, shall I not be like unto Enkidu? Sorrow has entered my heart. I am afraid of death and roam over the desert." What is the difference here?

REMARK: It is more personal.

Yes, but in what sense, for his grief over the lost friend was personal too. But in a special sense it is personal in that it hits back onto himself. It appears that he has to experience his friend's death on a still deeper level. Enkidu's death is becoming for him the experience of death as such. It seems that for the first time he has been struck by the awareness that man has to die and that this applies also to him. As a collective being, he had, of course, known it. He had seen people die, but up to now he had not fully realized it. I think that is something very general. We all have had such experiences of things which we knew long ago, but which suddenly hit us in a new way. It becomes a different experience; a new realization which had not been connected with it before. What we know and even have experienced earlier, may reveal its innermost meaning only in very special moments. I have heard, more than once, from women, that only with one child, a special one, did they suddenly realize what it meant to be a mother. They had had children before, but it did not change them inwardly. And so also, we have all had experiences connected with death, but *once* it becomes the archetypal experience, one could say. Every human archetypal experience gets its full weight only when it meets in us the maturity to receive and to understand it. I recall a case Dr. Jung once mentioned of a woman in a depression who complained that life was very monotonous, and that she never had experienced anything. Then it turned out that she had five children. Yet she never experienced anything. That can be true. It depends on what matrix there is to receive the experience. The question is whether the content is constellated to become conscious. Only if it is constellated to become conscious will we become fully aware. That also shows us that we are in a process of development. Not that different things happen to us outside, but that they happen to us differently inside. We have a new layer of inner existence where they hit us. And then they can open up, while at another time they do not.

So one can see this also here. Now he is hit. Not only by the loss of his friend, but by the realization that that can happen to him. Through Enkidu's death Gilgamesh becomes aware of death as a human reality. Enkidu's death is re-flected, as it were, onto Gilgamesh's human existence. This is expressed literally in Gilgamesh's reflection: "When I die, shall I not be like unto Enkidu?" There you can see that it never had occurred to him before. In realizing death Gilgamesh becomes human. His two-thirds divine substance have reached the human in him. Dr. Jung remarked in discussing this occurrence: "Gilgamesh, by this experience, has stepped out of the *status nascendi* (the state of becoming) in the mother." We talked earlier about this problem of *pueri aeterni* who, if they do not take the challenge and watch the clock, live in a chronic promise of their future. Only with the realization of death and the limit of time, does life become real. In one of his seminars Jung said: "Accepting death is the condition for reaching new life. If one does not accept death, one gets death." Because then it is not real life anymore. I think that is what this epic deals with. But we will see that it does not end with a solution, but is the beginning of a very deep quest. After all, this was a very ancient time, and the problem has been carried on in further religious development through the ages.

VII

THE "NIGHT SEA JOURNEY"

1. The Scorpion People at the Gate of the Mountain

Now in this real predicament, in this primeval human pain of being fated to die, a helpful ancestral reminiscence comes to Gilgamesh: he wants to meet his ancestor, Utnapishtim, who found eternal life. His name has in it the name of the old Sumerian sun god, Utu; and Napishtu is the soul. The Hebrew *nephesh, nefesh,* is the same word. *Nefesh* in Hebrew is also the term for the *anima vegetativa,* the vegetative soul, which is the life principle. So he has an ancestor who found eternal life. One human being, one of his ancestors has found what he is searching for, and to him he now feels driven. And immediately after this there begins what we may call the night sea journey of the hero who has become human.

In the night he comes to mountain passes where lions threaten him. Here he prays, not to Shamash but to Sin, the moon god, the light of the night in which he finds himself: "Also now, O Sin, preserve me!" At last he falls asleep, and has a dream. He sees beings who enjoy life in the moonlight.

He took his hatchet in his hand.
He drew the sword from his belt.
Like an arrow he fell among them.
He smote.... and broke them to pieces.

(Tabl. IX, col. i, lines 12, 15-18, Heidel p. 65)

Unfortunately, the designation of these beings in the text is damaged, so they could not be deciphered. Schott assumes that they were lions. As Gilgamesh had been threatened by lions there earlier, and had been afraid of them, this is not improbable; especially as he later relates no less than four times, in reporting on his painful journey, that he had killed lions in the mountains. The inner factors also speak in favor of this assumption: the lion, the animal of the desert, is also the animal of the underworld in the Babylonian concept, in which there exists a certain identity of desert and underworld. You remember that Nergal is a lion-god, and that Ereshkigal, the goddess of the netherworld, has a lion's head. The sun of the underworld comes to mind. Also the fact that the lion is sacred to Ishtar. In fighting against the lion with an axe, sword, and arrow, i.e., three symbols of discriminating consciousness, he overcomes, so to speak, the underworld into which he had been in danger of being drawn by Enkidu's death.

Gilgamesh continues on his way and comes to a mountain.

The name of the mountain is Mashu.
As he arrives at the mountain of Mashu,
Which every day keeps watch over the rising and setting of the sun,
Whose peaks reach as high as the "banks of heaven,"
And whose breast reaches down to the underworld,
The scorpion-people keep watch at its gate,
Those whose radiance is terrifying and whose look is death,
Whose frightful splendor overwhelms mountains,
Who at the rising and setting of the sun keep watch over the sun.
                    (Tabl. IX, col. ii, lines 1-9, Heidel p. 65)

Here Gilgamesh's journey of suffering begins also to become a cross for the interpreter. There are many symbols which cannot be fully explained, or even not at all. First, the mountain Mashu. The older scholars took it to be a geographical name. Jensen and Zimmern thought of the Lebanon and Anti-Lebanon. Gressmann considered it to be identical with the mountain Masis in the Syrian version of the saga of Alexander the Great. There Alexander comes to a mountain Masis after he has crossed the heavenly window of the sun and entered the land of darkness. Still today Masis is the name of the highest mountain in Armenian central Ararat district. But Böhl pointed out that Mashu is a Sumerian loan word, and means 'twins,' and in the Babylonian mythology the moon god has twins, whose names are Mashum and Mashtum, a man and a woman. Now the 'scorpion people' are a couple, husband and wife, who exercise the same function as the mountain – to keep watch over the rising and setting of the sun – so that they seem to be identical, or at least have mountain character, with their

Picture 9: The Scorpion People

heads reaching to heaven and their breast going down to the underworld, thus connecting the two. And they watch the way of the sun. Furthermore, the image of two mountains between which the sun sets and rises, is a motif which appears frequently on seal cylinders; and there are hymns found on seal cylinders, which describe the sun-god opening the doors of heaven and arriving on a great mountain where heaven and earth come together. If we associate the scorpion people with the psychological meaning of the zodiac sign of the scorpion, it makes good sense, for astrologically this is the sign of death and rebirth, *stirb und werde,* and this is the symbolical meaning and central issue of Gilgamesh's journey

*Picture 10: The Sun God Shamash ascending
between the two mountains*

through the mountain, to the other side. Scorpion men also appear in the *Enuma elish*, the Babylonian creation myth, among other monsters which Tiamat, the original mother goddess, created out of herself to fight Marduk:

She has set up the Viper, the Dragon, and the Sphinx,
The Great-Lion, the Mad-Dog, and the Scorpion-Man,

among others, and

With venom for blood she has filled their bodies.
Roaring dragons she has clothed with terror,
Has crowned them with haloes, making them like gods,
So that he who beholds them shall perish abjectly.
         (Tabl. II, lines 27-28 and 22-25, Speiser, ANET, p. 63)

The scorpion people in our text, "whose radiance is terrifying and whose look is death," make us think of the Gorgons, of Medusa. Our text goes on:

When Gilgamesh saw them,
His face became gloomy with fear and dismay.
But he took courage and approached them.
The scorpion-man calls to his wife:
"He who has come to us, his body is the flesh of gods!"
The wife of the scorpion-man answers him:
Two-thirds of him is god, one-third of him is man."
         (Tabl. IX, col. ii, lines 10-16, Heidel p. 65f)

She seems to know a little more than her husband, but they recognize the divine in Gilgamesh. This is the factor which enables him to stand their sight, and this is probably what revealed his divine quality to them. For, as in the Greek myth, just seeing the Medusa would kill the observer. Perseus was able to behead the Medusa only by looking at her reflection in his shield. Here too we have such a numinous horrifying archetypal being. Naturally, we could go on thinking it has to do with the terrible devouring mother which the hero here also has to meet, and we certainly would not be far off the track if at all. Many of the Greek myths come from, or were very influenced by those of Asia Minor. On the other hand, we need not insist that everything must be traced back historically, although where there are historical influences they have to be recognized, and they are helpful for our understanding. But the archetypes naturally can come up in very similar ways in widely separated times and places. But I do think that it is very likely that this motif, which had its hold on Asia Minor, influenced the Greek myth. Though it should be said that where there are influences, it also needs a time in which the theme is constellated. You can see that very beautifully in the Old Testament. There are lots of mythological images from Babylon and Canaan in the prophets or in the psalms and in the later literature, but on another level. When constellated, when the old image symbolizes a new content, then, usually, it is taken over. But we cannot go into this problem now.

It strikes me as very meaningful that Gilgamesh's divine character is stated at this very moment, just when he is in his most human situation, when he is in his lowest spot as a human being, hit by his experience of death. Through his union with Enkidu, and through Enkidu's death, Gilgamesh has become human. He had descended from his divine existence into human existence. But now he has to realize his divine character from his human existence as a starting point. The same thing happens in our human processes with the Self. You have to be very human to realize the Self, otherwise you are the Self, and in the worst case get a huge inflation, even a psychotic one. There is the need for this inner opposition, of the ego being aware of the divine in him, as the Self. He starts out as the Self. For instance, children, who have not developed an ego yet, are very close to the Self, and can say fantastically deep and wise things. But that state has to be lost and then regained, as it were. There is a Talmudic legend that an angel is present at the birth of every child, and the child has a candle burning on his head, a symbol of knowing everything. At the moment of birth, the angel blows out the candle and the child forgets everything – and has to regain it. In another version, the angel taps him on mouth, and the child falls into forgetfulness of all divine knowledge. Plato too, said that all knowing is remembering, which might also have been influenced by much older thoughts. But, in the very human situation, the divine as the Self becomes visible: the light shineth in the darkness. Behind the emphasis of Gilgamesh's divine character by the scorpion-man, is hidden the psychological truth that it is not the natural man going the way of the sun, but the divine in him. *That* is the *secundus homo*. It is no longer the instinctive man who is going on this journey. Therefore all experiences of spiritual life are, in some way or other, connected with a sacrifice by the instinctual man. So for instance, Jung explained the limping of Jacob after being touched in the hollow of his thigh by the man who wrestled with him all night at the ford of the Jabbok, to whom Jacob said "I will not let thee go except thou bless me." (Gen. 32:27). After that his name was changed to Israel, which means 'he who strives with God.' The change of name symbolizes a change in the person. Thereafter he limped, because that spirit touched him on the thigh. The thigh is often a symbol for the generative powers of man. That change symbolizes the experience at Jabbok, for which a sacrifice of the natural man is the price. That does not mean that the natural man ceases to exist, but the identification with the natural man stops. Just as with Enkidu, when he ends his experience with the hierodule. He is not then a spiritual person, but he is not identical with his animal nature any more. The scorpion-man next asks Gilgamesh:

> *Speaking these words to the offspring of the gods:*
> *"Why hast thou traveled such a long journey?*
> *Why hast thou come all the way to me,*
> *Crossing seas whose crossings are difficult?*

The purpose of thy coming I should like to learn."

> (Tabl. IX, col. ii, lines 18-22, Heidel p. 66)

When Gilgamesh tells him that he took all this upon himself in order to find Utnapishtim, his ancestor, and to ask him about death and life, the scorpion-man answers him:

"There has not yet been anyone, Gilgamesh, who has been able to
do that.
No one has yet traveled the paths of the mountains.
At twelve double hours the heart.....
Dense is the darkness and there is no light.
To the rising of the sun.....
To the setting of the sun.....

> (Tabl. IX, col. iii, lines 8-13, Heidel p. 66)

There are gaps here, but you get the idea that these mountains, the passage through them, has to do with the rising and the setting of the sun. But Gilgamesh does not let himself be deterred. In desperate determination – and this could almost be the motto of the whole Epic, he insists:

"Though it be in sorrow and pain,
In cold and heat,
In sighing and weeping, I will go!
Open now the gate of the mountains."

> (Tabl. IX, col. iv, lines 33-36, Heidel p. 66)

This is really an acceptance of all the suffering connected with the way of reaching the goal. And then the scorpion-man permits him to cross the mountains, and even wishes him a safe return.

2. Dense is the Darkness

We have already encountered this motif of a reversal of original opposition because of the steadfastness of Gilgamesh. First it was Enkidu, and then the elders, who tried to deter him from going on his way, and now it is the scorpion-man who says "What are you doing! No one has gone that way before. You cannot do it." But when he stands firm, the objection is withdrawn. Such opposition, it seems to me, is a sort of test, and a necessary one. Only he who cannot help it, who feels he must do it, may go this dangerous way. This is also applicable today: one should not be pushed into analysis. Sometimes a nudge is in place, but only when the fruit is ripe and waiting to fall from the tree. When people are just sent into analysis, it usually does not work. You cannot help anyone who does not feel he needs help. We will see this testing motif again in further episodes, with increasing importance.

Gilgamesh now enters through the mountain gate, and starts on the way of Shamash, "along the road of the sun," as the text informs us. A description follows which I feel to be a masterpiece of the archaic art of story telling, of which the whole epic is a wonderful example, but this passage seems to be especially beautiful and impressive. In connection with the artistic quality of the epic, some commentators talk of the poet or author as the genius who has written this story. It is clear that this is an old mythical narrative, or combination of narratives, and naturally in its written form it must have been set down by somebody. But it is precisely with archetypal material, rising from the unconscious, that people with an artistic capacity can write it out beautifully, but they did not create the material. That is a matter of gift, but not the matter of content. The material, the content, is 'written' by the unconscious first, so to speak, whence comes the inspiration for putting it, however artistically, into its spoken or written form. Naturally a great work of art can come right out of the unconscious of a genius, but in our case we know the story has been told and copied over ages. It is erroneous to give the impression that this is a story composed by a single author, although the arrangement of the originally disparate myths or parts of them, is, as we can see, a truly inspired creative accomplishment. An altogether congenial artistic spirit must have formed this great material. By the simple means of continuing repetition, Gilgamesh's way seems to be endless, until the first deviation in the narrative creates a certain relaxation, and the subsequent changes permit us to breathe freely together with Gilgamesh. I would like to read at least some parts:

> *One double-hour he traveled;*
> *Dense is the darkness and there is no light;*
> *Neither what lies ahead of him nor what lies behind him*
> *   does it permit him to see.*
> *Two double-hours he traveled.*
>
> (Tabl. IX, col. iv, lines 47-50, Heidel p. 67)
>
> .... [top broken off] ....
> *Four double-hours he traveled;*
> *Dense is the darkness and there is no light;*
> *Neither what lies ahead of him nor what lies behind him*
> *   does it permit him to see.*
>
> (Tabl IX, col. v, lines 23-25, Heidel p. 67)

This is repeated until after the seventh double-hour, then:

> *Eight double-hours he traveled, and he cries out;*
> *Dense is the darkness and there is no light;*
> *Neither what lies ahead of him nor what lies behind him*
> *   does it permit him to see.*
> *Nine double-hours he traveled, and he feels the north wind.*
> *........ his face.*
> *But dense is the darkness and there is no light;*
> *Neither what lies ahead of him nor what lies behind him*
> *   does it permit him to see.*

After he has traveled ten double-hours,
.... is close.
.... of the double-hour.
After he has traveled eleven double-hours, the dawn breaks.
                    [lit.: the glow of the sun has come out]
After he has traveled twelve double-hours, it is light.
Before him stand shrubs of precious stones; upon seeing them,
                    he went there directly.
The carnelian bears its fruit;
Vines hang from it, good to look at.
The lapis lazuli bears foliage;
Also fruit it bears, pleasant to behold.

(Tabl. IX, col. v, lines 35-51, Heidel p. 67f)

3. The Garden of Jewels

So finally, after this almost unendurable journey through the impenetrable darkness of the mountain Mashu, Gilgamesh comes out into a sort of garden of the gods where trees bear jewels as fruit, lapis lazuli and carnelian. What does that symbolize?

REMARK: A spiritual garden.

Why? Why jewels?

REMARK: They are treasures.

They are treasures, yes, and they also stand, because of their quality, for the imperishable. The diamond, for instance, is frequently a symbol for the Self, for the precious content, for the *corpus incorruptibile* of the alchemists. The imperishable quality of the fruits may suggest that they do not grow in a natural paradise. To enter here is perhaps connected with the obtaining of that *corpus incorruptibile*, which itself has to do with a recovery of primeval human perfection and splendor. This is to be seen in a very close parallel, Ezekiel 28:13. There Ezekiel speaks to the arrogant king of Tyre, and says:

> ... thou wast in Eden in the garden of God; every precious stone was thy covering, the carnelian, the topaz, and the emerald, the beryl, the onyx, and the jasper, the sapphire, the carbuncle, and the emerald, and gold; the workmanship of thy settings and of thy sockets was in thee, in the day that thou wast created they were prepared.

The king of Tyre was driven out of this jeweled garden of God, of paradise, because of his arrogance and guilt. For Gilgamesh it is only a transition. You would expect that ' *now,* here we are. Now we have reached it,' would be the situation. Here he is, as it were, in the situation of his immortal ancestor, but to our astonishment, he just passes through this garden and goes on to another adventure. He comes to Siduri, the innkeeper, who dwells by the edge of the sea. What does it mean that he only traverses this paradise? You know, we sometimes have such dreams of perfection. Young people can have such paradisical dreams, and what would it mean if they were to get stuck there, so to speak?

REMARK: In a sense, he was not fully conscious; not enough to appreciate it.

Yes, I would say it is something he must know is there, that something like this exists – but he has to go on to live his life. There is always this danger, this 'peril of the soul,' to get stuck in the divine, and not to come back. Therefore it is very important when doing active imagination to keep one's hold on to one's everyday human existence, otherwise one can be caught in the unconscious by its very beauty. You know that famous story of the Pied Piper who lured all the children into the mountain, and then the mountain closed behind them. The danger is always present that one can stay caught in the unconscious, fascinated by its beauty, and not go on living one's life. But why must he go there at all? I would say that such images come to us as an indication of another aspect of the world, another mode of existence we are moving towards, but we are not allowed to stay with them. One is happy to have such a dream because it gives one a positive orientation. They point to a possibility of realization which we are not yet up to.

I recall the dream of a young woman who had tremendous difficulties in relating to men. In the dream, she came into a flower shop. No one was there, and then she rang the bell. A very mundane ordinary start, you see. She waited a long time in the shop, and then the owner came down from above. She was an unusual, super-human woman, because she did not walk down the steps, but floated down. So she had a kind of angelic quality. And so she appeared before this young woman and told her no less than the four possibilities of how woman could relate to man. The dreamer *knew* it then, and woke up, and to her dismay, could not recall it. She was just desperate that she had forgotten what this divine woman had told her. It is as though the unconscious sometimes would tease us like this. But I think it is not a tease. With all her troubles and difficulties, she had to know that there is something like this, that in her is a Self figure who knows. Sometimes young troubled people get hints, for the sake of enduring and surviving until they can know. So they know that there is an inner order. They are not yet ready to experience it, but there is something, there is this treasure of archetypal knowledge of the depth of life. But we have to earn it. It is not put into our laps. I think something of this kind happens to Gilgamesh here. He is not meant, as far as one can see, to stay in this garden with the lapis lazuli fruit, and that is the end of it. Beautiful, but he was not there in order to remain there, so he goes on.

4. Siduri the Barmaid

He comes to the inn-keeper Siduri, who dwells by the edge of the sea. She prepares the divine potion for the gods, so in this sense is a kind of Hebe, the daughter of Hera and

Zeus, who was the cupbearer to the gods. In the lists of the divine names we find hers as one of the names of Ishtar. Our text tells us "She is covered with a veil." As the veiled Ishtar she is the bride, the maiden. According to some commentators that is the meaning of her name. She is also called Sabitu, which probably means inn-keeper. But according to another scholar, the Dutchman Th. C. Vriezen, both of these names contain the allusion to 'nymphs,' and he mentions that she also appears as a serpent-goddess and keeper of the herb of life and of the waters of life. That is very important in connection with the crucial incident later when a serpent takes the herb of rejuvenating life from Gilgamesh. Her character as maiden anima can be seen from her behavior on first seeing Gilgamesh, who is described as follows in the text:

> *Gilgamesh comes along and ....*
> *He is clad in pelts ....*
> *He has the flesh of gods in his body,*
> *But there is woe in his heart.*
> *His face is like unto that of one who has made a far journey.*

She becomes afraid, and:

> *She says to her heart and speaks these words,*
> *As she takes counsel with herself:*
> *"Surely, this man is a murderer!..."*
>
> (Tabl. X, col. i, lines 5-13, Heidel p. 71)

And she bars the door. But Gilgamesh threatens to smash it down unless she opens it. Here we can see the anima quality, here comes in something of the maiden meeting the unknown man. But behind her fear is more than the maiden's fear of the stranger. Gilgamesh really is a murderer. He felled the cedar, symbol of the mother, killed Humbaba, killed the heavenly bull, and lions in the mountain paths on his way. After she finally lets him in he tells her extensively of

all these deeds. But before that, as we can deduce from the
Old Babylonian Version, there was a strange interlude.
There is a large gap in the text in which apparently Siduri
must have given Shamash an account of Gilgamesh and the
last words describing his pitiful state are still preserved.
Whereupon the text continues:

> *Shamash felt distressed, he went to him,*
> *And said to Gilgamesh:*
> *"Gilgamesh, whither runnest thou?*
> *The life which thou seekest thou wilt not find."*
>
> (Tabl. X, col. i, lines 5-8, Heidel p. 69)

Now how do you like that? This is Shamash speaking, the
one who put Gilgamesh on his way! How can one understand
this? There are only two possibilities really. But first let us
hear Gilgamesh's answer, which is burning with a deep
spiritual longing.

> *Gilgamesh said to him, to valiant Shamash:*
> *"After walking and running over the steppe,*
> *Shall I rest my head in the midst of the earth*
> *That I may sleep all the years?*
> *Let mine eyes see the sun that I may be sated with light.*
> *Banished afar is the darkness, if the light is sufficient.*
> *May he who has died the death see the light of the sun."*
>
> (Tabl. X, col. i, lines 9-15, Heidel p. 69)

How can we understand that Shamash himself now tries
to deter Gilgamesh, and gets such a response? Is it just sort
of a fit of madness on the part of Shamash, as though he has
forgotten all that he had previously done? That would not
be impossible in light of what we can read about the ancient
ambivalent gods. It could happen. But such an assumption
is not quite satisfactory. Another possible assumption, especially in view of the previous attempts to deter him, is that
this too, is of the character of a test. We almost have to

assume so when it is Shamash himself, on whose way Gilgamesh is going, who tries to deter him from this very way. It is
as though he is making sure of his determination, because
what is to come is still more difficult. It happens in life quite
often that something new is constellated, and decided upon,
but then one succumbs to all kinds of counter considerations. 'Well, after all, maybe I really should not go.' Then
one really should not. As long as one can be deterred, it is no
time to go. One might even have dreams at a certain time,
taking an opposite view, and then the same proposition
comes up again from the unconscious.

It's a matter of the attitude of the ego. We should never
forget that when facing the unconscious, the counterpart is
the ego. How the ego faces the unconscious counts. We may
not think that we are here just to rely on the unconscious
alone. Sometimes people go so far as to say: 'I do not know
whether I can lunch with you tomorrow. Maybe I will have a
dream.' That goes too far. You have to make your own
decisions. Of course, that is a bit of an exaggeration, but
similar things happen. We have to relate to the unconscious,
but the unconscious is in a polar relationship with our ego,
and only what the ego can integrate can be realized. One
could almost say that when the unconscious sees that we are
wavering, or following too slavishly, it can take the proposal
away. Naturally, we may feel that we miss chances. What we
have to do is to *try* to be up to the unconscious. But if we are
not – as Jung once said: The unconscious is not altogether
human. It does not know what we can think. And sometimes
we have to tell the Self: 'But look here, I am only human,'
and to tell the unconscious, as it were, where our limits are,
because the divine has no limits. So it is really a dialectic
process, and only that leads to individuation. Identifying
with the unconscious does not lead to individuation. It
needs the relation of the ego to the unconscious. Jung says
in one of his seminars that an ego which is not complete,
does not know its circumference, (and the integration of the
shadow belongs here especially), and such an ego will have a

twisted relationship with the unconscious.

The task of the ego is to work at being as complete as it can. The security of its relationship to the unconscious depends on the *awareness* of the ego of itself and its state. The unconscious needs the answer of the ego; it is really a give and take, one could say, for the attitude of consciousness has an effect on the unconscious. Mythologically this shows in that the gods answer, if we come with a question. There are dreams which are clearly an answer to an ego which is really taking pains to understand the unconscious. I recall Jung's once saying to me in talking over a dream: "Only an analyzed person can have such a dream." Because it presupposes a certain work at oneself. So I could imagine, if we want Shamash not to be a wavering moody kind of god, and because we prefer to think that he was not, that there can be an unconscious purpose in his saying 'what are you doing? You can not do that.' And you saw what the answer of Gilgamesh was.

But his compassion for Gilgamesh, of which the text tells us, is also an explanation. The gods often do not know what they are doing to man in an unconscious urge, as it were. Here I come back to the possibility I mentioned before: sometimes a man can be destroyed by the divine challenge. One example is King Saul, in the Old Testament, as I have shown in my essay "King Saul and the Spirit of God." Or until he rebels against it, like Job. Job enters into an argument, telling God what he can take, and what not. But that this divine cruelty has its deep necessity is borne out precisely by the fact that Gilgamesh rejects the divine compassion. He does not want Shamash's compassion. He wants to see the light. He is already too much captivated by the mystery of Shamash to accept his compassion. All the pain he has to suffer in order to see the sun, is nothing compared to the pain which forced him on his way: darkness.

In the course of analysis people quite often get terribly afraid to go on. But they are in an in-between state. They do not want to go back either, because they have already reached so much; a dawning of something, or an awareness of something they cannot give up any more. But there are passages, painful passages, where people wish they could stop. Or if they do, they cut something off, and try to go on somehow. But very often you hear the complaint: 'I cannot stop anymore! I already know too much. But I almost feel I cannot go on either!' There one can only try to see what the Self wants. Naturally, you can always step out. It only depends on whether it was an inner necessity or an escape. These things are terribly real, and as you see, from the beginnings of time human beings began to develop a consciousness.

Now the talk with Siduri continues. She asks him, after he has told her about all his heroic deeds why he looks so downcast after he has achieved all that. Gilgamesh answers:

> *"He who went with me through all hardships,*
> *Enkidu, whom I loved so dearly,*
> *Who went with me through all hardships,*
> *He has gone to the common lot of mankind.*
> *Day and night I have wept over him.*
> *. . . . .*
> *Since he is gone, I find no life.*
> *I have roamed about like a hunter in the midst of the steppe.*
> *And now, O barmaid, that I see thy face,*
> *May I not see death, which I dread!"*
>
> (Tabl. X, col. ii, lines 1-13, Heidel p. 69f)

The answer of Siduri, who is really, we can say, an anima figure, is most significant:

> *Gilgamesh, whither runnest thou?*
> *The life which thou seekest thou wilt not find;*
> *For when the gods created mankind,*
> *They allotted death to mankind,*
> *But life they retained in their keeping.*
> *Thou, O Gilgamesh, let thy belly be full;*
> *Day and night be thou merry;*

Make every day a day of rejoicing.
Day and night do thou dance and play.
Let thy raiment be clean,
Thy head be washed, and thyself be bathed in water.
Cherish the little one holding thy hand,
And let the wife rejoice in thy bosom.
This is the lot of mankind....

(Tabl. X, col. iii, lines 1-14, Heidel p. 70)

Now what does she do? She conjures up before his eyes the inevitability of death as a common human lot. You have to die. And then she calls his attention to the pleasures of life. What is her aim? She wants to pull him back into a full natural life, to involve him again in the Epicurean *carpe diem,* 'pluck the day.' That is her advice, and it sounds terribly modern. 'Enjoy life as long as you can, for afterwards you will be dust under the earth.' Which is a discarding of all other aspects of inner values. One could say that this is the last word of the *material* culture; that is what the civilization of material culture has to say. And *materia* comes from *mater,* mother. Somewhere it is very seducing, is it not? Gilgamesh is really like a crazy man, emaciated, run down, suffering, and here he wants the impossible – he wants the divine life.

REMARK: I find it interesting that at the end of the story Shamash and Siduri are proved right in a way, because that is the end of a person's own possibilities.

Yes, you are absolutely right; you cannot have the divine life without accepting real life. He *has* to come to the acceptance of human limitations. He did not start out very humbly, as you remember. He was an inflated tyrant, and through Enkidu he grew into the heroic endeavor. But nevertheless, he had to go on, before being able to come back to so-called real life. Would he follow her advice now, it would be a regression, because then he would be coming back more or less the same as he had been before. That is always the seduction; why not just live naturally, like the flowers in the fields, and so on. But that too is nature which drives man to consciousness, and *that* is what he has to follow. But if he just wants to jump out and be divine instead of human, it will never work. Therefore he does not reach immortality on his terms. We will find out later what he brings back from this journey when he returns to Uruk. It would not, it could not go on with Gilgamesh, but it went on as a religious development in further time, reaching down to us; namely, this problem of life and death. It is good that you raised this question, for we must see the ambivalence in his search. On the one hand he is inflated, on the other he has a deep spiritual longing. We sometimes cannot differentiate that very well even with modern people. Because even in an inflated wanting to jump beyond oneself, there is a genuine something which wants to be nourished. It would be easy to tell, if it were not the archetype itself which inflates us. In every inflation there is an archetypal great happening, only the ego cannot stand it, and that is what makes the inflation. As Jung writes in Aion, inflation can occur by the ego enlarging itself like a balloon by identifying with the Self, or by a great content of the Self swallowing the ego. That is an accident. We cannot just say that someone is inflated. It is an accident if we become inflated, and we must be glad if we can come out of the balloon. But there is always a great content behind that which inflates, and we can at least hope to be able to stand and understand the content. To return to Gilgamesh's search; after a gap in the text we come to his penetrating question:

> "Now, barmaid, which is the way to Utnapishtim?
> What are the directions? Give me, oh, give me the directions!
> If it is possible, even the sea will I cross!
> But if it is not possible, I will roam over the steppe."
>
> (Tabl. X, col. ii, lines 16-19, Heidel p. 74)

5. Crossing the Waters of Death

The divine inn-keeper tries to make him see the impossibility of his undertaking:

"Gilgamesh, there has never been a crossing;
And whoever from the days of old has come thus far
                    has not been able to cross the sea.
Valiant Shamash does cross the sea,
                    but who besides Shamash crosses it?
Difficult is the place of crossing and too difficult its passage;
And deep are the waters of death, which bar its approaches.
Where, Gilgamesh, wilt thou cross the sea?
And when thou arrivest at the waters of death, what wilt thou do?
                    (Tabl. X, col. ii, lines 21-27, Heidel p. 74)

But then, in the midst of her speaking, a beneficial idea comes to her with an apparent change of mind, as occurred with previous attempts to deter him from going on his way.

Gilgamesh, there is Urshanabi, the boatman of Utnapishtim.
With him are the stone images, in the woods he picks...
Him let thy face behold.
If it is possible, cross over with him;
                    if it is not possible, turn back home."
                    (lines 28-31, Heidel p. 74)

Here the anima becomes, for the man who can stand her, the guide of his soul.

Urshanabi asks him, as Siduri did before, and with the same words, about the cause of his grief:

"Why are thy cheeks so emaciated, and why is thy face downcast?
Why is thy heart so sad, and why are thy features so distorted?
Why is there woe in thy heart?"
                    (Tabl. X, col. iii, lines 2-4, Heidel p. 75)

Gilgamesh tells him his story in all its details again, and begs Urshanabi to lead him to Utnapishtim. But he is told:

> *Thy hands, O Gilgamesh, have prevented thy crossing the sea;*
> *For thou hast destroyed the stone images."....*
>
> (lines 37-38, Heidel p. 76)

Now, what these stone images are, nobody can tell up to our days, as far as I can see. There are a lot of conjectures. Thompson thinks that they really were not stones but sails; Gressmann thinks of stone cases which were used in connection with the waters of death, which one was not allowed to touch. Others, and this hypothesis seems to me to be the most probable one, think of apotropaic stone images which were attached to the boat.* In any case they must have been necessary for crossing the sea, because Gilgamesh, who earlier smote them in his rage – we do not know why – must now, according to Urshanabi's instructions "go down to the forest and cut one hundred and twenty punting poles, each sixty cubits in length," in order to cross the waters of death. They board the ship and launch it, and on the third day, having covered what ordinarily took a month and fifteen days, they arrive at the waters of death.

> *Urshanabi said to him, to Gilgamesh:*
> *"Press on, Gilgamesh! Take a pole for thrusting.....*
> *Let not thy hand touch the waters of death....*
> *Gilgamesh, take thou a second, a third, and a fourth pole;*
>
> (Tabl. X, col. iv, lines 1-4, Heidel p. 77)

and so until he uses up all one hundred and twenty poles. Even those are not quite enough, for at the end he has to

---

* Editor's note: However see the plausible suggestion by Herman J. Finkel in "The Search for Dilmun," that they were loadstones (magnetite), which acted as magnets, enabling Urshanabi to find the north and thus to navigate the sea easily.

tear off his clothes and hold them up as a sail. Utnapishtim sees them coming.

> *Utnapishtim looks into the distance;*
> *He says to his heart and speaks these words,*
> *As he takes counsel with himself:*
> *"Why are the stone images of the ship destroyed?*
> *And why does one who is not its master ride upon it?*
> *The man who is coming there is none of mine....."*
>
> (lines 12-17, Heidel p. 77)

6. Utnapishtim the Distant

Again there is a gap in the text. Gilgamesh has reached Utnapishtim. Utnapishtim also first asks him the same questions as did Siduri and Urshanabi, and similarly, Gilgamesh answers: "Utnapishtim, should not my cheeks be emaciated and my face be downcast?" and goes on telling the story of his sufferings and the story of Enkidu's death, which he concludes by saying:

> *The matter of Enkidu, my friend, rests heavy upon me, so that far*
> *and wide I roam over the steppe;*
> *How can I be silent? How can I be quiet?*
> *My friend, whom I loved, has turned to clay; Enkidu, my friend,*
> *whom I loved, has turned to clay.*
> *And I, shall I not like unto him lie down and not rise forever?"*

But then he adds:

> *"That now I might come and see Utnapishtim, whom they call*
> *'the Distant,'*
> *I went roaming around over all the lands,*
> *I crossed many difficult mountains,*
> *I crossed all the seas;*
> *Of sweet sleep my face has not had its fill;*

I have wearied myself with walking around
*   and have filled my joints with woe.*
Not yet had I come to the house of the barmaid
*   when my clothing was worn out.*
I killed bear, hyena, lion, panther, tiger, stag, ibex, wild game,
*   and the creatures of the steppe;*
Their flesh I ate and their pelts I put on."

(Tabl. X, col. v, lines 19-32, Heidel p. 78f)

And now Utnapishtim, he who has found eternal life, also tries to make him acquiesce to the inescapable destiny of death for mankind.

"Do we build a house to stand forever?
Do we seal a document to be in force forever?
Do brothers divide their inheritance to last forever?
Does hatred remain in the land forever?
Does the river raise and carry the flood forever?
Only the dragon-fly sheds his cocoon,
Only its face will see again the face of the sun.
From the days of old there is no permanence.
The sleeping and the dead, how alike they are!
Do they not both draw the picture of death?
Whether he was a servant or a master, who can tell it after they
*   have reached their destiny?*
The Anunnaki, the great gods, gather together;
Mammetum, the creatress of destiny, decrees with them the destinies.
Life and death they allot;
The days of death they do not reveal."

(Tabl. X, col. vi, lines 26-39, Heidel p. 79)

Here again I feel the test-motif to be the underlying indispensable explanation for this homily. Utnapishtim, the Old Wise Man, has a secret, and he must investigate whether Gilgamesh is the right person to whom to reveal it. If Gilgamesh were to be deterred in his quest, he would be the wrong person.

VIII

THE SECRET OF THE GODS

1. The Divine Plot Betrayed

But Gilgamesh is not put off. He says:

"I look upon thee, Utnapishtim,
Thine appearance is not different; thou art like unto me.
Yea, thou art not different; thou art like unto me.
My heart had pictured thee as one perfect for the doing of battle;
But thou liest idly on thy back.
Tell me, how didst thou enter into the company of the gods and
obtain life everlasting?"

(Tabl. XI, lines 2-7, Heidel p. 80)

In the same way as the people of Uruk once stated the equality of Gilgamesh and Enkidu, Gilgamesh now states his equality with Utnapishtim. The former equality symbolized the connection of man with his animal side; the latter, with his divine side. To Gilgamesh's strange reproach on account of Utnapishtim's idleness I will come back later. Utnapishtim answers him:

"Gilgamesh, I will reveal unto thee a hidden thing,
Namely, a secret of the gods I will tell thee."

(Tabl. XI, lines 9-10, Heidel p. 80)

Thus it is the matter of nothing less than the divine secret itself, which can be revealed only to the chosen one. It is with this interchange that the famous 11th tablet of the Gilgamesh Epic, the prototype of the Biblical flood story, begins. The secret Utnapishtim reveals is nothing else than the flood story. Why it is the divine secret par excellence we will see from the narrative itself. Utnapishtim, the Babylonian Noah, is, as we know today, the hero of a formerly independent Sumerian myth, which was subsequently worked into the Gilgamesh Epic. In the Sumerian texts his name is Zisutra, which name became Xisuthros with a late Babylonian writer, Berossus. Here we can speak of a real process of melting things together in which the unconscious took part, for this narrative is connected with the previous text in a most meaningful way. In the 12th tablet of the Epic this is not the case, so we can appreciate all the more the organic connection of the 11th tablet with the whole epic. Now let us turn to the flood-story itself. Comparing it with the Biblical flood-story gives us the possibility of most valuable insights into a phase of religious development. Utnapishtim goes on to tell Gilgamesh how the gods were in the midst of Shurippak, an old city on the banks of the Euphrates:

> *Now their hearts prompted the great gods to bring a deluge.*
> *There was Anu, their father;*
> *Warlike Enlil, their counselor;*
> *Ninurta, their representative;*
> *Ennugi, their vizier;*
> *Ninigiku, that is, Ea, also sat with them.*
>
> (lines 14-19, Heidel p. 80)

No human guilt is mentioned here as being the cause of this disaster. On the contrary, Ea afterwards accuses Enlil of destroying mankind *without reflection,* instead of "putting the sin on the sinner." So it is divine incalculability and unpredictability which brings about the flood. Ea takes part in the

Picture 11: Tablet XI, the story of the flood

divine plot to destroy all mankind, but he at least wants to save one human being. We can see this by the ruse which follows, by means of which he advises Utnapishtim, who is sleeping behind the wall of a reed hut, to build a ship and save himself. He repeats the speech of the gods to the reed hut.

> *'Reed hut, reed hut! Wall, wall!*
> *Reed hut, hearken! Wall, consider!*
> *Man of Shurippak, son of Ubara-Tutu!*
> *Tear down thy house, build a ship!*
> *Abandon thy possessions, seek to save thy life!*
> *Disregard thy goods, and save thy life!*
>
> (lines 21-26, Heidel p. 80f)

So his idea is that *one* man at least should survive. If we compare this with the Old Testament flood story, we see that both these tendencies, the unpredictable decision to bring on the deluge, in which Enlil, the god of the earth, is in the foreground, as well as the other divine decision, personified by Ea, the god of wisdom, namely to save one man, are united in the Bible in the one ambivalent God personality, Yahweh. For He decides to "blot out man ..... from the face of the earth" (Gen. 6:7), and at the same time he rescues Noah. We can here follow a religious development 'in fla-grante' so to speak, putting the attributes of two separate gods into the one divine personality.

Concerning Ea's ruse to keep the divine secret and yet give it away, by the expedient of not revealing it to man directly, but to an object; we find the same motif in fairy tale and saga. There is the well known Grimm's fairy tale, The Goose Girl, who is not allowed to reveal that she is the real princess, but tells her secret to Falada, the decapitated horse's head which was hung over the gateway. It is over-heard in the kitchen of the palace, and afterwards everything has a happy ending. The conspiracy of Lucerne is a famous Swiss tale in which a little boy who knew the secret but was forbidden to reveal it to anyone, told it to a stove, and thereby the city was saved from the plotters. So we find this motif of telling and not telling also in our very old text. It is a ruse of Ea, the god of wisdom, who is on the side of mankind. He and Shamash have a lot in common. They are even mixed up once in our story. Shamash was reproached, you recall, for coming too close to mankind, for dealing with them as though they were one of his own. And here we have this leaning toward humanity which makes Ea save Utnapishtim, telling him, via the wall, to build a ship and to "Cause to go up into the ship the seed of all living creatures." The ship shall be of equal proportions, like Apsu which is the subterranean sweet-water ocean, the home of Ea, and in the Babylonian conception, the source of all sweet water. Utnapishtim listens respectfully, and then, out of a decent feeling, says to Ea:

> *'Behold, my lord, what thou hast thus commanded,*
> *I will honor and carry out.*
> *But what shall I answer the city, the people and the elders?'*
> (lines 33-35, Heidel p. 81)

As we will see, Ea does not share these human feelings for the inhabitants of Shurippak with Utnapishtim, but gives him the following advice, free of any moral scruples:

> *'Thus shalt thou say to them:*
> *I have learned that Enlil hates me,*
> *That I may no longer dwell in your city,*
> *Nor turn my face to the land of Enlil.*
> *I will therefore go down to the* apsu *and dwell with Ea, my lord.*
> *On you he will then rain down plenty;*
> (lines 38-43, Heidel p. 81)

This is again no lie, but the poor people have no idea of *how* it was going to rain. Here you see in Ea not only the human touch, but also the ruthlessness of the gods, who are not limited by anything. While he is interested in saving Utnapishtim, he has no scruples whatsoever in deluding the people with a story which will make them accept his leaving, and even give them a feeling that everything will be OK afterwards. There follows a long description of the building of the ark, with all details of measurement. It was one hundred and twenty cubits in each dimension, i.e., it was a cube, seven stories high, or deep. Very interestingly, Utnapishstim relates that:

> *Shamash set for me a definite time:*
> *'When the leader of the storm causes a destructive rain to rain*
> *down in the evening,*
> *Enter the ship and close thy door.'*
> *That definite time arrived.*
>
> (lines 86-89, Heidel p. 84)

But the tutelary god of Utnapishstim is Ea. This is the example I referred to earlier where Shamash is put for Ea, which shows that these two gods had a similar meaning. It also may point to there having been two versions originally. But the main thing is that it shows that Shamash also had been brought into connection with the rescue of Utnapishstim. This does not surprise us in the light of what we have learned before, namely, that rescuing from the flood is also an endeavor of rescuing consciousness out of the unconscious.

2. The Flood

And now follows the most vivid description of the flood itself:

> *As soon as the first shimmer of morning beamed forth,*
> *A black cloud came up from out of the horizon.*
> *Adad* [god of storm and rain] *thunders within it,*
> *While Shullat and Hanish go before,*

Coming as heralds over hill and plain;
Irragal [=Nergal, god of the underworld]
                    pulls out the mooring posts;
Ninurta [god of war and lord of irrigation] *comes along and*
                    causes the dikes to give way;
The Annunaki [judges in underworld] *raised their torches,*
Lighting up the land with their brightness;
The raging of Adad reached unto heaven
And turned into darkness all that was light.
.... the land he broke like a pot.
For one day the tempest blew.
Fast it blew and....
Like a battle it came over the people.
No man could see his fellow.
The people could not be recognized from heaven.

And now something extraordinarily interesting again,
from the point of view of religious history:

Even the gods were terror-stricken at the deluge.
They fled and ascended to the heaven of Anu;
The gods cowered like dogs and crouched in distress.
Ishtar cried out like a woman in travail;
The lovely-voiced Lady of the gods lamented:
'In truth, the olden time has turned to clay,
Because I commanded evil in the assembly of the gods!

She points to herself as the culprit for this disastrous
decision.

How could I command such evil in the assembly of the gods!
How could I command war to destroy my people,
For it is I who bring forth these my people!
Like the spawn of fish they now fill the sea!'
The Anunnaki-gods wept with her;
The gods sat bowed and weeping.
Covered were their lips....

(lines 96-126, Heidel p. 84f)

We see the gods are terror-stricken by their own unpredictability. What they did *happens* to them, as it were. One could almost say they happen to themselves. They are overwhelmed by themselves. But the most impressive passage is the lamentation of Ishtar, who calls herself the main culprit. When we recall her earlier behavior, something fundamentally new attracts our attention. What?

REMARK: When she wooed Gilgamesh who recounted all the terrible things she had done to her lovers, and then complained to her father, she exposed her shadow qualities, but there was no insight. Here there is.

Yes, it seems that there is a reflection; her own deeds reflect upon herself, in the literal sense, being bent back on herself. What is the faculty of insight? It is to be able to question oneself, to reflect on oneself, and that is really *the* basis for the growth of consciousness. Sometimes one sees people who are just not able to question themselves. Everything is projected to the outside. One can say it is a grace of God if we are *able* to question ourselves, to reflect upon ourselves. I warn you not to be too optimistic here about Ishtar. But nevertheless something new is happening in her, and if we take the former story as a comparison, we can say that there is even a hidden hint of a development in this deity, which could have to do with her defeat. Her power was broken through Gilgamesh, and that might have to do phenomenologically, with this rising faculty of being able to see something in herself. As long as it is unlimited, as Jung described it in the "Answer to Job," the divine power is not in need of consciousness. We all *mirror* each other, and very often this being mirrored helps us to see ourselves. If one lives in splendid isolation then one does not meet oneself; one is not forced to meet oneself. One does not get any reflex of how one affects others. These gods who suddenly are struck by what they themselves did, get afraid of themselves. This impact is the beginning of consciousness on the divine side. Ishtar expresses a certain amount of consciousness by saying 'How could I do that? What happened to me? What got into me?', so to speak. That could be a turning point to consciousness. She becomes a problem to herself; she is able to reflect on herself.

> *"How could I command such evil in the assembly of the gods!*
> *How could I command war to destroy my people!*
> *For it is I who bring forth (lit.: give birth to) these my people!"*
> (lines 120-122, Heidel p. 85)

There you see the ambivalence of the creative and destructive Great Mother, and this ambivalence begins to become a problem to her.

Looking at the Gilgamesh Epic as a whole, I cannot help thinking that this change in the image of Ishtar has something to do with Gilgamesh's development, for the state of consciousness also influences the unconscious. As already touched upon, there is a mutual relationship between the conscious and the unconscious, and when the ego takes a step, it has an effect on the unconscious. As I mentioned earlier, the dreams of people who are in analysis change quality after a while, because consciousness is collaborating, and is reflecting, and throws the ball back to the unconscious, which then comes up with another answer. Mythologically one could say that with human development, the gods also are transformed, and in this sense we can talk of a development of the God image, which we see in religious texts. Utnapishtim goes on telling:

> *Six days and six nights*
> *The wind blew, the downpour, the tempest, and the flood*
> *overwhelmed the land.*
> *When the seventh day arrived, the tempest, the flood,*
> *Which had fought like an army, subsided in its onslaught.*
> *The sea grew quiet, the storm abated, the flood ceased.*
> *I opened a window, and light fell upon my face.*

I looked upon the sea, all was silence,
And all mankind had turned to clay;
The ... was as level as a flat roof.
I bowed, sat down, and wept,
My tears running down over my face.
I looked in all directions for the boundaries of the sea.
At a distance of twelve double-hours there emerged a stretch of land.
On mount Nisir the ship landed.
Mount Nisir held the ship fast and did not let it move.

(lines 127-141, Heidel p. 85f)

3. The Post-Deluge Reaction of the Gods

Then the birds are sent out – here they are a dove, a swallow, and a raven; in the Bible the dove is sent twice – and after that the ark can be left. Just like Noah, Utnapishtim offers a sacrifice.

The gods smelled the savor,
The gods smelled the sweet savor.
The gods gathered like flies over the sacrificer.

(lines 159-161, Heidel p. 87)

Here again you have this kind of disrespectful portrait of the gods as being so greedy and jumping on the sacrifice. You know, this detail has gone over into the Bible; an especially illustrative archaic relic. In Genesis 8:21 we read:

And the Lord smelled the sweet savour; and the Lord said in His heart: "I will not again curse the ground any more for man's sake;...."

And in the following, you remember, He makes a covenant with Noah, and puts a rainbow in the sky as a token of remembrance, *in the first place for Himself,* that never again shall He bring a deluge. That is strangely overlooked in most

commentaries. It is not a sign for Noah but for *Himself!*
which shows that this ambivalent God-personality *needs* a reminder not to destroy mankind again. In just the same way,
Ishtar speaks:

> *As soon as the great goddess arrived,*
> *She lifted up the great jewels which Anu had made*
> *according to her wish:*
> *'O ye gods here present, as surely as I shall not forget the lapis*
> *lazuli on my neck,*
> *I shall remember these days and shall not forget them ever!'*
> (lines 162-165, Heidel p. 87)

So Ishtar can be recognized, if we are consequent, as an
aspect of the Godhead, Yahweh, Who has been melted together from a plurality of gods. I find this so very exciting
because through the comparison of the two stories we can
see the various moods of the one God, Yahweh, represented
by separate gods in the Babylonian epic. Seen from the
point of view of religious history, this seems to me to cor-
roborate the idea that the monotheistic God-personality
Yahweh, combines in Himself all those divine aspects which,
in polytheism, are not connected except by family relationships, partly. But only by this union in the one personality
does the ambivalence of the gods become a problem. That is
the *conditio sine qua non* for the development of consciousness. Namely, there must be one kernel, one instance, which
connects these different aspects. If a human being is totally
unconscious, all these inner figures which can appear in the
psyche, can take over, one after the other, and there is no
ego at home, so to speak, to know who is taking over. Once
one is angry, once one is in a good mood, and there is no
continuity. There is no one to reflect: *I* had a good mood, *I*
am gripped by wrath, or by love. There is no one to connect
it, or to feel that this happens to *me.* So it is the *one* personality
which I feel is the deepest inner necessity I can think of, for
religious development pushing into monotheism. Namely,

that the one God-personality, being the Self-image of human personality, is necessary for development. Otherwise we just are; one day it rains, one day the sun shines; they have nothing to do with each other. Then one is the pawn of the gods – unless one develops a center which is related to all these inner powers. That is what religion is all about.

As you know, according to Jung, etymologically and psychologically, the root meaning of religion is to carefully take into consideration the inner powers. The ego can know it is confronted with inner powers stronger than itself. It has to develop a relationship to all these deep divine aspects, good and bad. Otherwise it is just drifting. It is through this relationship that these powers can unite and change too. From the point of view of the development of consciousness, one can see this whole religious development of the god-personality in the light of the growth of consciousness. And Ishtar is, as it were, that aspect in Yahweh who represents on the one hand the divine unpredictability – which one can also see in other passages in the Bible – but on the other, who begins to change, that is, to realize and to limit her unpredictability. But what in the Bible became a new creation through the so-called first covenant with Noah, and the start of a whole salvation plan, here, as we will see, is not of too great consequence at that time. In what follows we witness the play of a veritable domestic quarrel among the gods. Ishtar, namely, wants to exclude Enlil from the sacrificial offering, which the gods have been missing for a long time. She says:

> 'Let the gods come near to the offering;
> But Enlil shall not come near to the offering,
> Because without reflection he brought on the deluge
> And consigned my people to destruction!'

(lines 166-168, Heidel p. 87)

What happened here? Ishtar apparently cannot stand her newly acquired self knowledge for too long a time. That can happen to human beings too. Insight can be lost again, and sometimes that has a very discouraging effect. But it makes all the difference that one had it once. Once, the sun did break through the clouds. Even if it should rain afterwards for a long time, one knows there is a sun, and it can break through. I think that is a consolation during periods when one is in a hole, as can happen during analysis. But if one has never seen it, it is a totally different situation. Here, Ishtar is only too glad to push off the main responsibility onto Enlil, who no doubt offers a great screen for projection. When he hears that Utnapishtim has escaped the flood, he becomes terribly angry at the Igigi, the gods of heaven. 'Has any of the mortals escaped? No man was to live through the destruction!' Ea, on whom suspicion falls that he may have given away the secret, defends himself:

> *'Moreover, it was not I who revealed the secret of the great gods;*
> *But to Atrahasis* [another name for Utnapishtim] *I showed a*
> *   dream, and so he learned the secret of the gods.*
> *And now take counsel concerning him.'*
>
> (lines 186-188, Heidel p. 88)

He says, 'please, I only sent him a dream. That is my business, to send people dreams. I did not give away the secret. But now it is done, so decide what you want to do about it.' And so Enlil has to cope with that *fait accompli*. Utnapishtim goes on speaking:

> *Then Enlil went up into the ship.*
> *He took my hand and caused me to go aboard.*
> *He caused my wife to go aboard and to kneel down at my side.*
> *Standing between us, he touched our foreheads and blessed us:*
> *'Hitherto Utnapishtim has been but a man;*
> *But now Utnapishtim and his wife shall be like unto us gods.*
> *In the distance, at the mouth of the rivers, Utnapishtim shall dwell!'*
> *So they took me and caused me to dwell in the distance,*
> *   at the mouth of the rivers.*
>
> (lines 189-196, Heidel p. 88)

I will not give you all the theories about where "the mouth of the rivers" is, because there is a great literature about it, but I do not think it's terribly important from the mythological point of view. It is the *distant* place.

4. The Secret of the Gods

Now why is this flood story called the *secret* of the gods? What does it tell? It tells of their unpredictable destruction of mankind with its human consciousness, which they had earlier created; of destroying what had been built. The primeval waters cover the earth again. But one mountain peak, here it is Mt. Nisir, on which the last man will be saved, is rising above the waters. One summit, here a symbol of the conscious mind, rising above the waters of the unconscious. This is the general motif of the various flood stories. In the Bible it is Mount Ararat; in the Indian story it is the Himalaya. The corresponding mountain peak of the Himalaya, interestingly enough, is still today called Naubandhanem, which means 'ship's anchorage.' The Greek flood hero, Megaros, fleeing from the flood, is guided by the cries of the cranes. He reaches a mountain top, which is therefore called Geranaia, which means 'crane mountain.' In another version of the Greek flood story the hero is called Deukalion, and he lands on Mount Parnassus. It is significant in our connection that the flood heroes are related to consciousness. Thus Duekalion is the son of Prometheus, who stole the fire from the gods, and the Indian flood hero is the son of the sun god, Catapatha Brahmana. It belongs, so to speak, to the divine secret, that the divine idea of *man* should not be forgotten. For if the flood had destroyed all mankind, the creation of man would have been just a divine idea which did not work out. So the gods destroy man, but *one* had to be saved for there is a purpose with man.

Thus the secret of the gods is man's rescue from the danger of themselves! Man had to be saved from the gods!

That's the secret. For the gods need man. If we take it psychologically, it means that man is created for taking care of the inner powers for the sake of consciousness. One can not conclude anything else here. We can see that in the archaic narration when the gods, hungry after not having had any nourishment during the time when mankind was destroyed, gather like flies over Utnapishtim's sacrificial offering, behind which, however, we can sense the whole depth of the idea. In the fifth tablet of the Babylonian creation myth, the *Enuma elish*, it is said that man was created for the purpose of caring for the gods. And there the sacrifices are meant. But Marduk creates man out of the blood of the god Kingu, and Kingu was a rebellious god. So the gods planted this rebelliousness into man, as a challenge for themselves, as it were.

In contrast to the Biblical Noah, with whom a new consciousness begins, Utnapishtim is, as we see, removed to the gods. Here I would like to come back to that strange little incident, to the problem of Gilgamesh's accusation of Utnapishtim on account of his inactivity: "Thou liest idly on thy back." It is very difficult to understand this reproach, but I will tell you what I feel about it. You see, with Utnapishstim the human consciousness was saved, but it returned to the unconscious, as an archetype, as it were. He is living away from the world, at the mouth of the rivers, in the distance. He was called the distant one. That does not lead on, on the conscious human side. It is as if the archetype of man as such was rescued in the archetypal world, as though to wait for the time when it could materialize or be realized again. I feel this disappointment in Gilgamesh, something of 'what good are you doing *here*?' It does not lead to a creation or to a further development of mankind. One could say Utnapishtim is the archetype of the deified man, but he is not yet realized in the human world. For a lot of things happen mythologically among the gods, and a lot is in storage for future development. But if Utnapishtim is moved away he is not seen from the human point of view, only as a divine idea

of mankind which was once made real and then taken back
– and now one must wait for what may happen. He is, at
most, a reminder for the gods that they once created him, so
that they might be inspired for a new creation. Actually
there is a fragment telling that the gods, when Utnapishtim
was removed, immediately started to create a new mankind
in order to get their offerings. Gilgamesh is a second divine
attempt. He is one who wants the immortality, and would
like to get it, like Utnapishtim. And here another differen-
tiation becomes clear. To Utnapishtim it simply happened
that he became divine. He did not know how, and he was
not a searcher. He just had a dream, and Ea told him "you
had better pack up, leave everything, build a ship, and go."
Gilgamesh is a man who is hit by the reality of death, and
therefore looks for immortality. For Gilgamesh it is a *problem,
the* human problem par excellence.

5. Seven Loaves – the Failed Test

But how does it go on with him? When Utnapishtim
finishes telling him how he had been given eternal life, he
says to Gilgamesh:

> *But now as for thee, who will assemble the gods unto thee,*
> *That thou mayest find the life that thou seekest?*
> *Come, do not sleep for six days and seven nights.*
>
> (lines 197-199, Heidel p. 88)

This means that *contra naturam* – contrary to nature – he
should overcome unconsciousness. Naturally he is not up to
this task, and immediately falls asleep, prompting Utnapishtim to say to his wife:

> *"Look at the strong man who wants life everlasting.*
> *Sleep like a fog blows upon him."*
>
> (lines 203-204, Heidel p. 89)

To prevent Gilgamesh from later disclaiming that he had slept, Utnapishtim has his wife bake loaves of bread each day and put them at his head, to prove to him that he has slept through seven days. That this was a necessary procedure we see by what happened when Utnapishtim woke him on the seventh day. Gilgamesh says:

> *"Hardly did sleep spread over me,*
> *When quickly thou didst touch me and rouse me."*
> *Utnapishtim said to him, to Gilgamesh:*
> *"... Gilgamesh, count thy loaves of bread!*
> *The days which thou didst sleep may they be known to thee."*
> (lines 220-224, Heidel p. 89)

Gilgamesh is in great distress. He says to Utnapishtim:

> *"Oh, what shall I do, Utnapishtim, or where shall I go,*
> *As the robber has already taken hold of my members?*
> *Death is dwelling in my bedchamber;*
> *And wherever I set my feet there is death!"*
> (lines 230-233, Heidel p. 90)

So nothing can be changed. Gilgamesh has to return. But before he does, something new happens, which is worth mentioning because of its rebirth symbolism. Utnapishtim tells Urshanabi:

> *"Take him, Urshanabi, and bring him to the place of washing;*
> *Let him wash his long hair clean as snow in water.*
> *Let him throw off his pelts and let the sea carry them away,*
>   *that his fair body may be seen.*
> *Let the band around his head be replaced with a new one.*
> *Let him be clad in a garment, as clothing for his nakedness.*
> *Until he gets to his city,*
> *Until he finishes his journey,*
> *May his garment not show any sign of age,*
>   *but may it still be quite new."*
> (lines 239-246, Heidel p. 90)

There are some parallels for the symbolism of new garments as a sign of rebirth, of renewal. One is the Babylonian myth of Adapa, in which a new garment together with the food of life is offered to him in heaven (which he erroneously declines). Another is the Biblical episode in Zechariah 3:4ff., where God instructs the angel before whom the high priest Joshua is standing, to "Take the filthy garments from off him" and to replace them with robes. Urshanabi already wants to lead Gilgamesh back, when compassion wells up in Utnapishtim's wife, his ancestor mother. She says to her husband:

> *"Gilgamesh has come hither, he has become weary,*
> > *he has exerted himself,*
> *What wilt thou give him wherewith he may return to his land?"*
> > (lines 259-260, Heidel p. 91)

This causes Utnapishtim to reveal a second divine secret to Gilgamesh. He says:

> *"Gilgamesh, thou hast come hither, thou hast become weary,*
> > *thou hast exerted thyself,*
> *What shall I give thee wherewith thou mayest return to thy land?*
> *Gilgamesh, I will reveal unto thee a hidden thing,*
> *Namely, a secret of the gods will I tell thee:*
> *There is a plant like a thorn....*
> *Like a rose its thorns will prick thy hands.*
> *If thy hands will obtain that plant, thou wilt find new life."*
> > (lines 264-270, Heidel p. 91)

Immediately Gilgamesh knows what to do, which gives us the earliest known description of diving:

> *He tied heavy stones to his feet;*
> *They pulled him down into the deep, and he saw the plant.*
> *He took the plant, though it pricked his hands.*
> *He cut the heavy stones from his feet,*

And the ... threw him to its shore.
Gilgamesh said to him, to Urshanabi, the boatman:
"Urshanabi, this plant is a wondrous plant,
Whereby a man may obtain his former strength.
I will take it to Uruk, the enclosure, I will give it to eat ...
                    may cut off the plant.
Its name is 'The old man becomes young as the man in his prime.'
I myself will eat it that I may return to my youth."

(lines 272-282, Heidel p. 91f)

In his most valuable monograph on the sagas of the tree of life and the water of life, August Wünsche has shown that the herb of life is another symbolic form of the tree of life. There are different examples in Babylonia itself. In a collection of Assyrian letters we find the sentence: 'We were like dead dogs, which our lord, the king (meaning Marduk) brought to life again, by putting the herb of life under our noses.' The herb of life is the panacea, the healing herb, the *elixir vitae*, the *quinta essentia*. This also fits in with the literal meaning of a Babylonian word for the herb of life, namely, *samu balati*, plant of life, medicine of life. In Syriac the word *sam* also means medicament, poison, as in Hebrew, *sam* means drug, poison. This plant here is not for immortality, but for the renewal of youth, an old longing of mankind. On his way home with his precious find Gilgamesh stops one night and seeing a pool of cold water, enters it to bathe, when

A serpent perceived the fragrance of the plant;
It came up from the water and snatched the plant,
Sloughing its skin on its return.

(lines 287-289, Heidel p. 92)

6. Loss of the Plant of Rejuvenation

So the serpent got the renewal which Gilgamesh had anticipated eating "that I may return to my youth." Here we see him overcome by pain and deep disappointment at the loss of the wonderplant. He weeps bitterly, and the whole heroic effort seems to have been in vain.

> *"For whom, Urshanabi, have my hands become weary?*
> *For whom is the blood of my heart being spent?*
> *For myself I have not obtained any boon.*
> *For the 'earth-lion' have I obtained the boon."*
>
> (lines 293-296, Heidel p. 92)

The earth-lion is, of course, the serpent, which here is a symbol of the unconscious life. It is a very manifold symbol. Through the sloughing of its skin the snake has become a symbol of transformation and renewal. In this episode, the possibility of renewal, of rebirth as a kind of immortality, symbolized by the herb of life, which has come near to consciousness, has been swallowed back by the unconscious. Gilgamesh is not yet ripe, one could say; the mankind represented by him, is not yet up to getting immortality. But *this* kind of immortality he was not supposed to get at all. His only image of immortality is the image of a prolonged life. And *this* image is taken away from him, and as I see it, had to be taken away, to make room for a further development. This whole occurrence appears in a rather strange light if we connect it with the idea that Siduri-Ishtar, the watcher over the herb of life and the waters of life, was a serpent goddess. So we may assume that it was the mother goddess taking the herb of life away from him. But she becomes changed by it. One could say that a change occurred in the unconscious, which later is evident in Gilgamesh when he returns to Uruk, accompanied however, by Urshanabi, a living witness of Gilgamesh's journey to Utnapishtim. When they arrive he tells him:

7. Return to Uruk

"Urshanabi, climb upon the wall of Uruk and walk about;
Inspect the foundation terrace and examine the brickwork,
                    if its brickwork be not of burnt bricks,
And if the seven wise men did not lay its foundation!
One shar is city, one shar orchards, one shar prairie; then there
                    is the uncultivated land of the temple of Ishtar

(lines 303-306, Heidel p. 93)

He is proud of his work, but his pride is no longer that of the ambitious, power-driven ego of the beginning. In his description of the wall, which is identical with that of the narrator's introduction, he refers to the seven wise men (good spirits of a kind, who are also mentioned in other texts), who lay the foundation of Uruk, and he refers to the fourfold division of the city, which psychologically can be seen as an allusion to divine participation and to totality. And with this, that is, with the eleventh tablet, the Gilgamesh Epic really comes to its end.

The twelfth tablet is the second part of a Semitic version of a quite different Sumerian story which has nothing to do with the events of the preceding tablets. In the first part of the original story Ishtar, or Inanna as she is called in the Sumerian text, has plucked an uprooted *huluppu*-tree from the waters of the Euphrates, and planted it in her holy garden in Uruk, intending to have a throne and a bed from its wood when it grew thick enough. But by then a serpent had made its nest in the roots, the Anzu bird put its young in the crown of the tree, and in the trunk, the demon Lilith had made her dwelling, and they would not leave, to Ishtar's distress. Then Gilgamesh came to her help. He struck the serpent with his axe, and the Anzu bird flew to the mountains with its young, and Lilith fled to the desert. With the help of the sons of Uruk Gilgamesh cut off the branches, and from the trunk of the tree carved a throne and a bed for Ishtar. In return, Ishtar gave him two implements which she carved from the roots and the crown of the tree respectively, a *pukku* and a *mikkû*, which Heidel translates as drum and drumstick. To Gilgamesh's great distress these implements fell into the underworld one day. He wants to recover them, but cannot reach them. It is with his lamentation over this happening that the twelfth tablet of our Gilgamesh Epic begins. He says:

> *"Now, who will bring the* pukku *up from the underworld?*
> *And who will bring the* mikkû *up from the underworld?"*
>
> (Tabl. XII, lines 4-5, Heidel p. 95)

And now Enkidu declares himself ready to go down to the underworld and to fetch them for him. You can see from this that the 12th tablet is not consequent with the foregoing epic since Enkidu, who is here described as Gilgamesh's servant, not as his friend, did not perish, but is still alive. In the underworld Enkidu did not heed Gilgamesh's instructions on what not to do, and "the underworld seized him" and did not allow him to come up again. Gilgamesh pleads with the gods for his release, and finally Enkidu's spirit is permitted to come up to tell him the ways of the underworld. The different reasons for Enkidu's death in the two myths is striking. In the epic he dies from an ailment, in the Sumerian text of the 12th tablet it is an accident which brings him to the underworld, which he then cannot leave. Yet this is the 12th tablet of the Gilgamesh Epic, glued onto it, so to speak, and we must ask ourselves what meaning this could have. The tablet ends with a comfortless picture of the underworld described by Enkidu.

8. The Meaning of the Epic

When Gilgamesh returns to Uruk after the loss of the wonder herb, it seems at first glance to be merely a return to the beginning. Has his journey been in vain? I do not think so. He did not find the eternal life which he hoped and longed for. But through the inner experiences on his journey when searching for immortality he changed. He must now submit to 'the ways of the underworld,' to death. Therefore his wanting to know, through Enkidu's spirit, about the laws of the underworld:

> *"Tell me, my friend; tell me, my friend;*
> *Tell me the ways of the underworld, which thou hast seen."*
> (Tabl. XII, lines 87-88, Heidel p. 99)

This seems to be the next task, for which, it seems, he is only now ready; for he has seen Utnapishtim, he came to know "the secret of the gods," and found the herb of life. He saw the light he longed to see, and felt the spirit which he had missed. This makes the loss of the herb of life appear in another light. It is not just a tragic 'misfortune' but perhaps, as already mentioned, a hint that he was not allowed to keep the herb of life, that the unconscious denied it to him because, though it would have meant rejuvenation and prolongation of life, which was the goal of his longing, it would not have meant a change of the inner man, corresponding to the deeper longing for illumination and enlargement of consciousness for which Shamash, the sun god, had chosen him. Desperation over death had led him seek a way to get around death by eternal prolongation of life on earth, but now the serpent in him also sloughed its skin. He picked up his life on earth again, accepting and including death. The two thirds god submitted to human existence, and the one third man experienced the divine.

The Gilgamesh Epic as a whole shows in its inner structure a process of transformation in the collective unconscious, an anticipation of the individuation process, represented in the hero. At the same time, it mirrors a significant era in the history of religion, a time when the Great Goddess Ishtar was defeated by the hero under the aegis of Shamash, the archetype of consciousness. This marks the beginning of the transition from polytheism to the monotheism of the Bible.

Gilgamesh, in accord with the heroic role, did step into the future, far ahead of the consciousness of his time. But the people was 'touched' by this heroic tale full of suffering. It became dawning and promise, which is the deepest meaning of all mythic tradition, which creates the necessary connection between man and the eternal realm of the archetypes.

SOURCES OF ILLUSTRATIONS

Cover: Gilgamesh – a giant bas-relief of the lion-conquering hero as guardian of the palace of Sargon II.

Frontispiece: Gilgamesh holding a lion; from the Khorsabad Sculpture.

Picture 1: Lilith, clay plaque, Mesopotamia, Old Babylonian Period, ca. 2000-1600 B.C.; Paris, Louvre, AO 6521.

Picture 2: A carved ivory; a lady [perhaps a cult woman] at her window; courtesy of the British Museum.

Picture 3: Lovers embracing on a bed, representing the cult of the sacred marriage, an annual event in Mesopotamian cities. Clay plaque, Mesopotamia, Old Babylonian Period, ca. 2000-1600 B.C.; Basel, Erlenmeyer Collection.

Picture 4: Humbaba; courtesy of the British Museum.

Picture 5: Radiant Inanna (Ishtar); cylinder seal, Mesopotamia; Akkad Period, ca. 2334 - 2154 B.C., black stone, 4 cm x 2 cm; courtesy of the Oriental Institute, University of Chicago, A 27903.

Picture 6: Enkidu fighting the heavenly bull; Akkad Period, ca. 2300 B.C., stone; in *Das Gilgamesch Epos* by Hartmut Schmökel, W. Kohlhammer Verlag, Stuttgart.

Picture 7: The Fight with the Bull of Heaven; in *Het Gilgamesj Epos* by F. M. Th. de Liagre Böhl, H. J. Paris, Amsterdam.

Picture 8: Enkidu 'verscheurt' the heavenly bull; Musea voor Kunst en Geschiednis, Jubelpark te Brussel.

Picture 9: The Scorpion People, lapis lazuli, 41mm x 17mm, New Babylonian, 600 B.C.; in *Das Gilgamesch Epos* by Hartmut Schmökel.

Picture 10: The Sun God Shamash ascending between the two mountains; impression from a cylinder seal; in *Het Gilgamesj Epos* by Böhl.

Picture 11: A section of the cuneiform tablet XI about the flood, first enciphered by George Smith; the British Museum.

BIBLIOGRAPHY

Albright, W. F., "Gilgamesh and Engidu, Mesopotamian Genii of Fecundity," *Journal of the American Oriental Society,* 40, 1920, pp. 307-35.

— "The Goddess of Life and Wisdom," *American Journal of Semitic Languages and Literatures,* 36, 1920, pp. 258-94.

— "The Name and Nature of the Sumerian God Uttu," *Journal of the American Oriental Society,* 42, 1922, pp.197-200.

Amiet, Pierre, "L'homme oiseau dans l'art mésopotamien," *Orientalia,* 21, 1952, pp.149-167.

— "Le Problème de la Représentation de Gilgameš dans l'Art," M. P. Garelli, *Gilgameš et sa Légende,* Paris, 1956, pp. 169-73.

Autran, Charles, *La femme et la courtisane,* Paris; Libraire Orientaliste, 1937.

Barlach, Ernst, *Der Tote Tag,* Berlin, 1912, 2nd edn., 1918.

Barton, George A., "A New Babylonian Parallel to a Part of Genesis 3," *Journal of the American Oriental Society,* 39, 1919, p. 287.

Baumgartner, Walter, "Das Nachleben der Adonisgärten auf Sardinien und im übrigen Mittelmeergebiete," *Archives suisse des traditions populaires,* 43, 1946, pp. 122-48.

— "Herodots Babylonische und Assyrische Nachrichten," *Archiv Orientální*, 18, 1950, pp. 69-106.

Baynes, H. G., Unpublished manuscript in the library of the Psychologischer Club, Zürich.

— "On the Psychological Origins of Divine Kingship," *Folklore*, 42, 1936, pp. 74-104.

Böhl, F. M. Th. de Liagre, "Das Gilgamesch-Epos bei den Alten Sumerern," *(MVEOL) Mededelingen en verhandelingen van het Vooraziatisch- Egyptisch Gezelschap / Gerootschop "Ex Oriente Lux,"* 7, 1947, pp. 145-77.

— "Die Fahrt nach dem Lebenskraut," *Archiv Orientální* 18, 1950, pp.107-22.

— "Mythos und Geschichte in der Altbabylonischen Dichtung," *Opera Minora*, 1953, pp. 217-33.

— "Das Problem Ewigen Lebens im Zyklus und Epos des Gilgamesch," *Opera Minora*, 1953, pp. 234-62.

— "Zum Babylonischen Ursprung des Labyrinths," *Opera Minora*, 1953, pp. 324-38, 509-12.

— "Die Religion der Babylonier und Assyrer," *Christus und die Religionen der Erde*,[2] ed. by DDr. Franz König, Vienna; Verlag Herder, 1956, pp. 443-98.

— *Het Gilgamesj Epos*, Amsterdam; H. J. Paris, 1958.

Chase, Richard, *Quest for Myth*, Baton Rouge; Louisiana State University Press, 1949.

Contenau, Georges, *L'Épopée de Gilgamesh, Poème babylonien,* Paris; Artisan du Livre, 1939.

— *La Vie Quotidienne à Babylone et en Assyrie,* Paris; Librairie Hachette, 1950.

Dhorme, Edouard, *Les Religions de Babylonie et d'Assyrie,* Paris; Presses Universitaires de France, 1949.

Ebeling, E., *Tod und Leben nach den Vorstellungen der Babylonier,* Berlin und Leipzig; Walter de Gruyter & Co., 1931.

—　　　　　"Liebeszauber im Alten Orient," *Mitteilungen der Alt-orientalischen Gesellschaft*, Band i, Heft 1, 1925, pp.195-208.

Falkenstein, S. A. und von Soden, W., *Sumerische und Akkadische Hymnen und Gebete*, Zurich; Artemis,1953.

Finkel, H. J., "The Search for Dilmun," *The Mariner's Mirror*, 62, 3, 1976, pp.211-33.

Fish, T.,　　"The Zu Bird," *Bulletin of the John Rylands Library*, 31, 1948, pp. 162-71.

Furlani, Giuseppe, "Das Gilgamesch-Epos, Eine Einführung," *Das Gilgamesch-Epos*, ed. by Karl Oberhuber, Darmstadt, Wissenschaftliche Buchgesellschaft, 1977.

Gaster, Theodore H., *Myth, Legend, and Custom in the Old Testament*, New York and Evanston; Harper and Row, 1969.

Grimm Brothers, "The Spirit in the Bottle," *Grimm's Fairy Tales*, London; Routledge and Kegan Paul, 1948.

Häfker, Hermann, "Zum Verständnis des Gilgamesch-Epos," *Das Gilgamesch-Epos*, ed. by Karl Oberhuber, Darmstadt; Wissenschaftliche Buchgesellschaft, 1977.

Hastings, James, ed., *Encyclopaedia of Religion and Ethics*, New York; Charles Scribner's Sons, 1908 - 1926.

Haupt, Paul, "Istar's Azure Necklace," *Beiträge zur Assyriologie und semitischen Sprachwissenschaft*, 10^2, 1927, pp. 96-106.

Heidel, Alexander, *The Gilgamesh Epic and Old Testament Parallels*, Chicago; The University of Chicago Press, 2nd Ed., 1949.

Herodotus, translated by George Rawlinson, London, 1862. Reprinted, New York; Tudor Publishing Company, 1928, 1956.

Hooke, S. H., *Babylonian and Assyrian Religion*. London, 1953.

—　　　　　*Middle Eastern Mythology*, Baltimore; Penguin Books, 1963.

Hurwitz, Siegmund, *Lillith, die erste Eva,* Zurich; Daimon Verlag, 1980.

Jacobsen, Thorkild, "How did Gilgameš oppress Uruk?" *Acta Orientalia,* 8, 1929, pp. 62-74.

Jensen, Peter, *Das Gilgamesch-Epos in der Weltliteratur,* Strassburg; K. J. Trübner, 1906.

Jung, C. G., (The letters CW refer to *The Collected Works of C. G. Jung,*) Bollingen Series XX, New York; Pantheon Books,

—   English Seminar, Winter, 1931.

—   "The Spirit Mercurius" in CW 13, 1948.

—   "Concerning Rebirth" in CW 9i, 1950.

—   "The Psychology of the Child Archetype" in CW 9i, 1951.

—   "Answer to Job" in CW 11, 1952.

—   *Symbols of Transformation,* CW 5, 1956

—   *Aion,* CW 9ii, 1959.

Kapelrud, Arvid, S., *The Violent Goddess,* Oslo; Universitetsforlaget, 1969.

Kluger, Rivkah Schärf, *Satan in the Old Testament,* Evanston; Northwestern University Press,1967.

—   "King Saul and the Spirit of God," *Psyche and Bible,* Zurich; Spring Publications, 1974.

Kraeling, Emil G., "Xisouthros, Deucalion and the Flood Traditions," *Journal of the American Oriental Society,* 67, 1947, pp.177-83.

Kramer, Samuel Noah, "The Epic of Gilgameš and its Sumerian Sources. A Study in Literary Evolution," *Journal of the American Oriental Society,* 64, 1944, pp. 7-23.

—   *From the Tablets of Sumer,* Indian Hills, Colorado; The Falcon's Wing Press, 1956.

— "Sumerian Literature and the Bible," *Studia Biblica et Orientalia,* 3, 1959; pp.185-204.

— *Sumerian Mythology,* (revised) New York; Harper and Brothers, 1961.

— and Wolkstein, Diane, *Inanna, Queen of Heaven and Earth,* New York, Harper & Row, 1983.

Landsberger, Benno, "Einige unerkannt gebliebene oder verkannte Nomina des Akkadischen," *Wiener Zeitschrift für die Kunde des Morgenlandes,* 56, 1960, pp.109-29.

Langdon, Stephen, "The Epic of Gilgamesh," *Pennsylvania Museum Journal,* 8, 1917, pp. 29-38.

Luckenbill, D.D., "The Temple Women of the Code of Hammurabi," *American Journal of Semitic Languages and Literatures,*34, 1917, 1; pp.1-12.

Matouš, Lubor, "Die Entstehung des Gilgamesch-Epos," *Das Altertum,* 4, 1958, pp.195-208.

— "Les Rapports entre la Version Sumérienne et la Version Akkadienne de L'Épopée de Gilgameš," P. Garelli, ed., *Gilgameš et sa Légende,* Paris; Librairie C. Klincksieck, 1960; pp. 83-94.

Meissner, B., *Babylonien und Assyrien,* 2 vols., Heidelberg; Carl Winters Universitätsbuchhandlung, 1920-24.

Morgenstern, Julian, "On Gilgamesh Epic XI, 274-320: A contribution to the study of the role of the serpent in Semitic mythology," *Zeitschrift für Assyriologie,* 4, 1929, pp. 284-300.

Mowinckel, Sigmund, "Wer war Gilgameš?" *Acta Orientalia,* 15, 1937, pp. 141-60.

— "Zur Göttlichkeit des Gilgameš und zur Entstehungszeit des Gilgameš-Epos," *Acta Orientalia,* 16, 1938, pp. 244-50.

Oberhuber, Karl, ed., *Das Gilgamesch-Epos,* Darmstadt; Wissenschaftliche Buchgesellschaft, 1977.

Opitz, Dietrich, "Der Tod des Humbaba," *Archive für Orientforschung,* 5, 1928, pp. 207-13.

Oppenheim, A. Leo, "Mesopotamian Mythology II," *Orientalia,* 17, 1948, pp. 17-58.

— "The Interpretation of Dreams in the Ancient Near East," *Transactions of the American Philosophical Society,* Philadelphia; New Series, Vol. 46, Part 3, 1956, pp. 177-373,

Popliche, Joseph, "A Sun Myth in the Babylonian Deluge Story," *Journal of the American Oriental Society,* 47, 1927, pp. 289-301.

Quiring, Heinrich, "Die 'heilige' Siebenzahl und die Entdeckung des Merkur," *Altertum,* 4, 1958, pp. 208-14.

Schmidtke, Friedrich von, "Gilgameschs Streben nach Erlösung vom Tode," *Morgenland,* 28, 1936, pp. 7-23.

Schmökel, H., *Das Gilgamesch-Epos,* Stuttgart; Kohlhammer-Verlag, 1966.

Schneider, Nikolaus, "Die Religion der Sumerer und Akkader," *Christus und die Religionen der Erde[2],* ed. by DDr. Franz König, Vienna; Verlag Herder, 1956; pp. 387-446.

Schneider, Vera, *Gilgamesch,* Zurich; Origo-Verlag, 1967.

Schott, A., *Das Gilgamesch-Epos,* Stuttgart; Reclam-Verlag, 1934.

— und von Soden, W., *Das Gilgamesch-Epos,* Stuttgart; Reclam-Verlag, 1958.

Smith, George, "The Chaldean Account of the Deluge," Lecture to The Society of Biblical Archeology, Dec. 3, 1872. But see his *Chaldean Account of Genesis,* printed in 1876, photographically reproduced by Wizards Bookshelf, Minneapolis, 1977.

Smith, Sidney, "The Face of Humaba," *Annals of Archeology and Anthology,* 11/3, 1924, pp.107-14.

Speiser, E. A., *"Enuma elish,* (The Creation Myth)," in Pritchard, James B. (ed.), *Ancient Near Eastern Texts Relating to the Old Testament,* 2nd ed., Princeton; Princeton University Press, 1955, pp. 60-72.

— "The Epic of Gilgamesh," in Pritchard, James B. (ed.), *Ancient Near Eastern Texts Relating to the Old Testament,* 2nd ed., Princeton; Princeton University Press, 1955, pp. 72-99.

Stamm, J.J., "Das Gilgamesch-Epos und seine Vorgeschichte," *Asiatische Studien, Zeitschrift der Schweizerischen Gesellschaft für Asienkunde,* 1/4, 1952, pp. 9-29.

Thompson, R. Campbell, *The Epic of Gilgamesh,* London; Luzac & Co., 1928.

Thureau-Dangin, F., "La passion du dieu Lillu," *Revue d'Assyriologie,* vol. XIX, 1921.

— "Chumbaba," *Revue d'Assyriologie,* 22, 1925, pp. 23-26.

Tigay, Jeffrey H., *The Evolution of the Gilgamesh Epic,* Philadelphia; University of Pennsylvania Press, 1982.

Ungnad, A., and Gressmann, H., *Das Gilgamesch-Epos,* Gottingen; Vandenhoeck & Ruprecht, 1911.

Virolleaud, Charles, "La Montagne des Cèdres dans les Traditions de l'ancien Orient," *Revue de l'Histoire des Religions,* 101, 1930, pp. 16-26.

— "Le Voyage de Gilgamesh au Paradis," *Revue de l'Histoire des Religions,* 101, 1930, pp. 202-15.

— "Le Dieu Shamash dans L'Ancienne Mesopotamie," *Eranos Jahrbuch,* Vol. 10, Zürich; Rhein-Verlag, 1944, pp. 57-79.

Wolkstein, Diane and Kramer, Samuel Noah, *Inanna, Queen of Heaven and Earth,* New York, Harper & Row, 1983.

Wünsche, A., *Die Sagen von Lebensbaum und Lebenswasser, altorientalischen Mythen,* Leipzig; E. Pfeiffer, 1905.

INDEX

ENGLISH PUBLICATIONS BY **DAIMON**

Susan Bach – *Life Paints its Own Span*

E.A. Bennet – *Meetings with Jung*

George Czuczka – *Imprints of the Future*

Heinrich Karl Fierz – *Jungian Psychiatry*

von Franz / Frey-Rohn / Jaffé – *What is Death?*

Liliane Frey-Rohn – *Friedrich Nietzsche*

Aniela Jaffé – *The Myth of Meaning*
　　　　　　– *Was C.G. Jung a Mystic?*
　　　　　　– *From the Life und Work of C.G. Jung*
　　　　　　– *Death Dreams and Ghosts*

Siegmund Hurwitz – *Lilith – the first Eve*

Verena Kast – *A Time to Mourn*
　　　　　　– *Sisyphus*

James Kirsch – *The Reluctant Prophet*

Rivkah Schärf Kluger – *The Gilgamesh Epic*

Rafael López-Pedraza – *Hermes and his Children*
　　　　　　　　　　– *Cultural Anxiety*

Alan McGlashan – *The Savage and Beautiful Country*

Gitta Mallasz (Transcription) – *Talking with Angels*

C.A. Meier – *Healing Dream and Ritual*
　　　　　– *A Testament to the Wilderness*

Laurens van der Post – *A «Festschrift»*

Jungian Congress Papers:

Jerusalem 1983 – *Symbolic and Clinical Approaches*

Berlin 1986 – *Archetype of Shadow in a Split World*

Paris 1989 – *Dynamics in Relationship*